Becoming Whole

How to Pick up Your Broken Pieces and Be Who You Were Born to Be

Kaneesha,

Sending all my healing vibes ♥

Heather Falter

HEATHER FALTER

CONTENTS

Dedicated to you. The one holding your broken wing.

INTRODUCTION

Hi friend. Yes, since you've picked up this book, you're now my friend! From my very first sentence to my very last, I hope you can feel from me how much I care about you. This book is truly dedicated to you.

I need you to know that I see what you are up against. You picked up this book with a girl holding her broken wing for a reason. Something about the cover resonated with you. She's broken, yet standing tall. She knows pain, difficulty, and temporary defeat.

She's also determined the story doesn't end here. She's determined to not let go of what once was lost. She's determined to not give up; to keep walking; to figure out how to put her broken parts back together. Her 'broken-ness' is not a sign of defeat, but proof of her growing strength.

Before I say another word, I hope you resonate with this image. I hope you see yourself in it. Since you're alive and moving around on this planet, I think it's safe to say that you've been through your fair share of heartaches, disappointments, and regrets. I'm going to assume that somewhere, somehow, you have been bruised and broken; that you have emotional scar tissue that you walk around with regularly.

Since you're holding this book, I also assume that you're ready to figure out how to heal all of those broken things. Something deep inside you knows that there is more to life than this; more to walking around as half of yourself.

Something gnaws at you, begging you to become who you were born to be. I'm here to help you do just that.

Becoming Whole is a book meant to help you step back and look at yourself as a whole. When we experience some sort of trauma, whether it be divorce, financial ruin, abuse, natural disaster, or any other thing, we tend to see only that thing. *Becoming Whole* is a reminder that there is so much more that makes up who we are. When we tend to ourselves *as a whole,* we are better equipped with the tools we need to heal. *You need all of you to become fully and joyfully you.*

The process of becoming whole is not about perfection. Perfection is an illusion. Trying to achieve it can drive us crazy! Instead, it is about waking up all of our parts and using them to the best of our abilities. Becoming whole is not about erasing the pain. Instead, you will learn that the only way out is through. Every life lesson you find along the way will become a jewel to carry with you.

Let me remind you that no matter what you are going through, the sun will shine again. You are loved, and you will find *joy.* While perfection and lack of struggle are not part of this book, joy is. I truly believe that you can and will find joy if you continue moving forward.

This book is made up of 3 parts: Part 1: The Pain; Part 2: The Work; Part 3: The Joy. I believe these 3 things are a cycle. We will go through each of them repeatedly throughout our lives as we spiral upward to becoming our best selves. The trick is to not get stuck in the pain, and to keep moving to experience joy. The more quickly we can feel the pain and do the work, the more time we are able to spend feeling joyful.

Part 3 is a discovery, a personal inventory, if you will. If you feel broken in your life, this is where I will help you to identify where exactly you are breaking. Is it your mind? Is it your heart? Is it your relationships? Is it your body? Finding that part and nourishing it is where you will start to feel the joy again. You'll find a lot of questions in this part. Take your time to pause and do a bit of soul searching. Be gentle with yourself. No one is perfect! Let your answers be a bit messy. We are all a bit messy. It's okay! As you go through each section, you'll find healing practices to adopt. These are a few ideas to get you started. It is only the beginning, and I believe the best answers will come from within you as you read. Mark up this book. Download and print my Becoming Whole Journal if you want to follow along with your own self-discovery.[1] And remember, no matter how defeated you might feel in any of these areas, stick with me till the very end. Your happiness awaits you.

Also, it won't take long in reading before you discover my faith in God. If you believe differently than me, *it's okay*! We can still be friends, and you still belong here with me. Feel free to insert whoever or whatever you believe in here. If you believe in nothing but the power of goodness or kindness somewhere out there in this universe, no matter how bleak, that is all you need to stay. Hope, even just a glimmer, is all you need. So cozy up, grab yourself some tea, and stick with me.

I promise you, no matter how broken you may feel or how messy your life is right now, if you continue doing your work of picking up these pieces, there will come a day when you will look back on your life and all you've been through with awe and gratitude. There will come a day when you are no longer burdened by the weight of your current sorrows. There will come a day when you'll think of the hard times and won't want to trade a second of them because of what they have made of you.

There will come a day when you won't even recognize your new self because of the strength you will have. You will experience *joy*. You will feel whole, not because everything is perfect and your life is pain-free, but because you are using your whole self to go about this big adventure of life.

But first, the pain...

PART 1
THE PAIN

I'm not sure when it happened; I'm not sure how or why. I'm not sure if I was born this way or became it through the pain. All I know is God has given me a taste of His love. It is a special and tender love that burns especially strong for anyone struggling.

- Heather Falter

1

MY STORY

've known from the beginning that this chapter would be the hardest to write. I wish I could jump ahead and tell you *how* I've overcome things without ever telling you *what* I've overcome. I'd love to package it up in pretty teachings, wrap it with a bow, hand it over, and curtsy. Unfortunately, I'm not that kind of person. If I'm going to write a book, I'm going to do it with my whole heart. So, in this chapter, I'll be handing over some pieces of my heart.

It's not easy to take this walk through my past for a lot of reasons. One, it was a long time ago, and quite frankly, I've moved on. These aren't things I still think about. Honestly, it takes a concerted effort to even remember them. Two, I deeply love every person that has been a part of my life, especially my parents. I mean that. I love them dearly and I don't hold anything against anyone anymore, so I don't enjoy writing about the trauma from our past. And three, I know that with any story there are details that we all experience differently. I know every member of my family could write their own book on their own experience. Honestly, I wish they would! Nonetheless, here we are. I know I want to write this book. I feel like *I need to write this book*. I truly want to use the trials I've faced to help you overcome yours. I don't know any other way to do that than to first tell you my story.

So, here it goes…

My name is Heather. My maiden name initials were H.A.M. so naturally, my family called me "Hammy," or "Hamster," or "Hairy Heather Henderson". (Insert embarrassed emoji here!) Dad called me his "Little Princess," and my friends called me "Scary Spice". Yes, we were the Spice Girls. No, I was not cool enough to know who they were when my friends were all shouting out their pick! (Mel B, I love you!)

When I was little though, I was "Heather Feather". That one fit. I remember being a pretty tender-hearted kid. I was sensitive and extremely shy. It was scary for me to talk to anyone outside of our immediate family when I was little. I still remember clinging to mom's legs and burying my face when anyone made the attempt to connect with me.

I was terrified to go to kindergarten. I still remember sneaking my blanket in my backpack and unzipping a hand-sized hole and rubbing it between my fingers as I walked home from school! (Ok, nowhere in this book will I be claiming to be cool.) I had dolls and bears and journals and all the introverted nerdy stuff.

I was the middle child, with two older sisters and two younger brothers. My youngest years were spent side-by-side with my middle sis. She wasn't much older than me and I liked having her close. The girl loved adventure and seemed to have no sense of fear. Before I was born and before she could even walk, she was climbing on top of very high things, including our refrigerator. She was always sporting her quirky smile as proof she didn't know she was being naughty! She and I spent our childhood battling over whether we played Barbies or Babies, dressing up our younger brothers as girls, and dancing on top of tables in our basement (probably much too provocatively for our age) singing songs at the top of our lungs! Middle sis was the quirky one, sporting around the house whatever silky sweet nothings she could find and living life with almost all her wild hairs intact. I felt braver when I was with her. I loved having her by my side.

As I grew, my oldest sister became my idol. She was 5 years older than me, and I followed her everywhere. All through elementary school and junior high I wanted to be her. I would wake up early to sit in her room and watch her get ready for the day. I would sit by her bedside, hanging on to any word she was willing to tell me about her friends and her life. I'd sit on her feet as she did her ab workouts. I'd clean her room. I would do anything for her! She may not have known, but in my eyes, she was my best friend—my very first hero. She never made me feel 'less-than' because I was younger. I remember feeling included by her. She was a cheerleader, so pretty, and everything I wanted to be. She taught me how to do my first back handspring. She taught me about music and boys and makeup. She taught me about life. Some of my most pivotal life moments were with her.

I'll never forget one night being in her room. I was probably in there sleeping on her floor. (We all had our own rooms, but hated sleeping in them!) That night the lights were out, and it was quiet. Out of nowhere, she broke the silence with laughter. I asked her what she was laughing about. Between giggles, she said, *"Oh, I heard this joke today, and I was just telling God about it!"* She continued laughing harder until we both were laughing. I'm sure she thought nothing of it and fell asleep after that. I didn't. I would bet money that if I called her right now, she wouldn't remember that night, but I do. I had heard a lot of prayers before, but that night *my oldest sister taught me how to pray.*

My parents are good parents. They loved us and taught us good values. They taught us to work hard and play hard. Dad taught us about money and the dangers of getting into debt. Mom taught us to clean like champions. They both taught us to work. We spent a lot of hours as a family out in the yard weeding the garden and cleaning out the garage on Saturdays. Summers smelled like freshly cut grass and water fights from the pool out back.

We had a lot of fun together. We spent the hottest months white water rafting, camping, and cliff jumping. We all loved to swim. We were the family known for our green hair, colored from too much chlorine buildup in our 90's bleached blonde style. People knew me from a mile away. Strangers would walk up to me and say, "You're a Moss, aren't you?" When I said "Yes", they would respond, "I can tell. You all look alike." Being in my family gave me a sense of belonging. I've always been proud of our name. We had a close-knit group of cousins and a grandma who never wavered. I remember climbing on her lap as she read scriptures to me. We never skipped reading and praying before bed when we stayed the night at Grandma's. I can still hear her voice and the melodious way she spoke as she read.

We were all good kids with good Christian values. Mom was the one who made most of the effort in that department. I remember her putting together little family lessons. She would be giving it her all, talking about God and Jesus with puppets and songs and activities to go along with it. We were very organized, each person doing their part, always holding hands in a circle as we prayed.

Usually, during these intricately prepared lessons, Dad would be sprawled out, snoring on the floor. Church-related things tended to have that effect on him! He was the dad with the line across his forehead at church because he spent the meeting with his head on the pew in front of us! (Sorry Dad, you know it's true!) He played along the best he could, but it was obvious to all of us that it wasn't really his thing. As kids, I think we thought it was funny. We would tease him about the forehead line, but from my young eyes, this seemed to be the first sign of him and Mom drifting apart.

Despite all of Mom and Dad's good efforts with us, there was a lot of conflict between the two of them. It seemed to come on slowly, but I can still remember sitting at the bottom of the stairs at night as they fought, clinging to my blanket that was soaked in tears. I'll never forget those nights. I was young then, but I still knew what was coming.

I often had dreams and inklings that they were going to split. Even at a young age, I had this sixth sense. I could feel things coming sometimes long before they happened. I remember saying to my mom, "You and Dad are getting divorced, aren't you?" She looked startled and did the best she could to answer my question. She comforted me and told me, "No." She said, "Fighting is normal and healthy" and that she wasn't going to give up. She promised that our family would stay together. I knew she meant that. I knew she wanted that. Still, I knew better.

"It's not supposed to be this way," I often thought. Something deep within me believed there had to be more to life than the struggle behind our family's closed doors. I longed to leave. I think God was preparing me.

I have one vivid memory toward the end of their marriage. I was at my best friend's house, two doors down from ours. The doorbell rang, and she told me to answer it. It was her boyfriend, standing still, wide-eyed, and pointing at my house. I spotted the red and blue lights swirling almost as fast as my heart began to race. Sprinting toward my home, I watched my mom, laying on a stretcher, being loaded in the back of an ambulance. Her arms were bandaged up, and there was blood. I asked the EMTs if she was going to make it. "We can't say." was their reply. I watched in horror as they pulled away, not knowing if I would see her again. I ran through the front door and fell into my oldest sister's arms. The scene inside left a feeling of horror deep in the pit of my stomach that I didn't know would be my constant companion for years to come.

Mom had said she was sad before. I knew she talked of not wanting to go on, but she had never attempted anything like this. She had been betrayed and was engulfed in her own pain. She said she didn't mean it; that she was only looking for love, which honestly only confused me more. I knew there was conflict between my parents, but this time it was different. What happened afterward was very much a blur.

Sister brought me over to the couch. I laid my head on her lap. Hot tears were rolling down the side of my face. I felt like I was floating, and part of me was not inside of my body.

"It's over," my dad told us, "and you'd better find a place to stay." Shortly after, we lost the house and everything I had ever known to be our family. At age 15, leaving our childhood home, all I can remember is this one thought hitting me like a ton of bricks- "I need to figure this out on my own."

I stayed with a friend for a while. She drove me to and from my lifeguard training at the city pool. I was glad there was water there. It hid the tears the best it could, and I could blame the chlorine for the red in my eyes.

The nights on her floor were long. It was there that I mastered the art of crying quietly. While Mom was in the hospital, we weren't allowed to visit. I don't remember how long she had to stay for treatment and monitoring, but it seemed like a while, and I was glad. I didn't want to see her.

Looking back now, I know that the day I watched her leave in the ambulance, I had to face that I might not see her again. This idea repeated in my mind that even if she made it this time, there were no guarantees of how long she would choose to stay. I came to terms with the fact that I needed to prepare to figure my life out without her. I didn't trust her and my young brain led me to the conclusion that I couldn't hang on to anyone too tight. Loving anyone seemed like an empty pit that would ultimately end in darkness. It became a pattern of thought for me that if someone was going to go, I'd rather be the one to leave.

The morals that once were important to our family no longer held their significance. No one seemed to care anymore, and in many ways, we were left to fend for ourselves morally, financially, emotionally, and mentally. And while I always managed to find a roof to be over my head, without these things I felt deeply homesick and homeless.

Living without parental guidance meant I was left to experience the world for myself. Like many kids in my situation do, I turned to alcohol to numb my pain. I spent the next 3 years within a figurative arms reach of a bottle, becoming dependent on the blessed source of liquid comfort.

Still, to this day, I'm unsure of whether drinking alcohol at this time of my life was a mistake. It got me through. It let me laugh. It let me cry. It helped me overcome some of my shyness. It helped me to think about something else and relax around my friends. I felt more comfortable with it in my veins.

For the first time in my life, I could talk to boys without wanting to run and hide. Everything seemed to be better with it. Alcohol became my trusted companion. It was a companion that wore off and made my head want to explode, but still, it was reliable. I didn't want to be without it.

The problem with alcohol is that while it helps to mask one problem, it becomes a whole new problem of its own. I learned that I didn't have to deal with my emotions anymore. I could take a swig, and the sting would begin to fade. I didn't have to think about anything or resolve my pain. Instead, I continued for the next few years to allow it to be my medication. On it, I wasn't the same.

I couldn't see myself changing. I didn't see a problem with it until I was out overnight with some friends. One of these friends had been there all along. We grew up together, and she knew me through and through. She had never been much of the religious type, although I tried my hardest to convert her as a kid! This same friend that *I* had been trying to tell about God since we met, looked at me, seemingly very disappointed, and said, "Heather, you need God." She watched me that night do things I never thought I'd do.

By this time, I had already lived with my sister and was now living in an empty house that my dad was renting. I hadn't seen him in a while. I went home that day, still buzzing from the night before. I walked into my weird 70's orange bathroom and stared at my face in the mirror for a long time. I just stood there, frozen with her words echoing in my ears. It was then that I realized I didn't recognize myself. The longer I stood and stared, the more my face seemed to morph into a hollow, creepy skeleton that wasn't me.

I don't know how long I was there. If I close my eyes, I can still see her. What terrified me the most was not that I couldn't recognize my own face. It was that the girl taking up space inside of me wasn't me. It was the most uncomfortable feeling I have ever felt, to be a stranger to the person inside of my own skin. I spent the next long while sobbing on the shower floor.

I wish I could tell you that I stopped drinking. I didn't. I tried, but I didn't. Part of it was because boxed wine and Vodka was all we had in our fridge. Part of it was because alcohol has its way of hanging on tight.

Eventually, and by the grace of God, I graduated high school. I honestly don't know how I did it. I found out a few days before graduation that I could walk with my class. I'm pretty sure someone in heaven pulled some strings because there was no way. My birthday is in August, so I was one of the youngest in my class. I was always trailing behind my friends' milestones, and this felt no different. I'm just glad it happened.

Most of them stuck around after graduation. I, on the other hand, ran as fast and as far away as I could. I got into massage school and moved south of my hometown right after graduation. I remember I needed special permission from the apartment to lease to me before I turned 18, and I felt like an idiot getting it. Strangely enough, the apartment was for a religious school with a strict no-alcohol policy. Sounded nice in theory. I still wasn't convinced it was a good idea.

Hidden within my boxes of clothes were bottles of my best friends, and I just so happened to not have to share a room. My middle sister had moved back from a school further south, and she helped me get into her same apartment complex. She was my friend by day, and those blessed bottles kept me company at night.

Having Middle Sis around was different. She was still the carefree, happy one. I liked being around her because she still seemed so innocent, and in my mind, she seemed so unaffected (although I'm sure she carried her own pain.)

Still, she smiled, had friends that smiled and did weird things like hanging out sober. The first few times I was around them, I was so confused. I didn't remember how to be around people without a buzz. I was awkward and quiet and wanted to crawl out of my skin.

Still, I liked them. I wouldn't admit it at first, but I wanted what they had. I spent a long time in yo-yo, pretending to be like them, and then sneaking away to find people who would help me get what I still wanted. I was confused. Living in between was worse than living all the way. My conscience was pleading with me to choose a better path. For the life of me, I couldn't muster the strength to do it.

One night, I felt especially conflicted about who I was. I stayed in that night and decided I'd be better off numb. I reached under my bed only to find a box that I had forgotten was there. This box was filled with memorabilia from my childhood that hadn't yet found a place with me in my new apartment. I smiled as I looked through pictures I had forgotten about; images of my nieces, who once gave me so much purpose and hope. I pulled out each piece, one by one, as if they each held secret clues as to who I really was. Then, like a ton of bricks, I spotted something that stopped me dead in my tracks.

At the bottom of that empty box was a book from my childhood. It was a book of scripture that my grandmother used to read to me.[2] I stood frozen, eyes glued, standing over that box as if I had actually seen a ghost. I was too terrified to pick it up. I didn't know what to do. I was equally afraid to pick up that book and start reading as I was to continue living my life half-alive. I knew I was at a crossroads.

As I was about to close the box and kick it out of sight, two thoughts entered my mind: one, "What would Grandma think of me if she could see me now?" and two, "I've been a member of this church my whole life and I have no idea what that book says." These two thoughts gave me the courage to pick up that book and start reading—a moment of courage that would ultimately alter the remainder of my life.

Reading was awkward at first. I didn't understand everything. All I knew was my heart was aching, and I needed help. I was hungry to feel something, anything, that would tell me I was going to be okay.

Learning about God was different than I thought. I'll be honest—I was terrified to know anything. Yes, I went to church when I was a kid—when I was innocent. But this was different. *I was different.* I didn't know what to expect, but I assumed reading the book would make me feel like I was screwed. I thought of the religious people I knew and assumed what they would think of me. I figured that was exactly what God would think of me too. I had no idea how wrong I was.

The book was about ancient people living in the Americas and their experiences and communications with God. They spoke differently than we speak now, but what they said meant very little compared to what I felt. I was surprised that instead of feeling shame, for the first time in a long time, I felt hope.

Again, I wish I could tell you that magically I found Jesus, gave up the liquor, and we all lived happily ever after. We didn't. I didn't. I promised myself 100 promises that I would stop, but it wasn't that easy. In fact, I made some of the biggest mistakes of my life while living in that apartment complex—things that I still shudder to think about. What happened instead was my life became this stark contrast of light and dark. It was as if, through reading, life seemed more clear to me. I knew one thing for sure—*I wanted to be in the light.* Little by little, as I read and spent more time with the right people, I started feeling more comfortable with them. Inch by inch, seemingly insignificant choices led up to big changes that eventually loosened alcohol's grip on me.

Some people go to AA meetings, I read my book. That is the honest truth. I get that that might not be everyone's answer, but it absolutely was mine. I took my book everywhere. The more I read, the more I wanted to read. I started waking up early to get a few chapters in before work. I snuck it in my bag just in case there was time to open it somewhere unexpected. I remember on my lunch break at work knowing I could either go in the break room and eat or go outside and read. I chose the latter more often than not. Everything was second to reading, including sleep and food.

I still didn't want to talk about it. I still didn't want anyone to see what I was reading. I couldn't help but fall in love with this idea that there was a God; that He knew me by name; that He had a plan for my life. I read things that said that *we were here to experience joy.*[3] I read in amazement that brave men stood for Christ, regardless of the consequences.[4] I wept on my bed when I read about what evil men did to the women and children who believed.[5] There were stories of good and evil, light and dark, righteousness, and wickedness.[6] There were warnings of pride and the reminder that we are all equal before God.[7]

Again, more than what I read was what I felt. I felt *love.* Before picking up that book, I was convinced that God couldn't love me. Real love seemed hard to come by, and I was sure that I wasn't qualified for it. *I didn't understand that God knows how to love better than humans do.* I didn't know that He doesn't think like they do, or feel like they do, especially about me personally. For the first time in a long time, I felt like somebody could see me. I felt like I was okay and that life would be okay. I wanted so badly to believe that there was a Savior who could heal me. Little did I know He had already begun doing just that. While picking up that book and rekindling the faith I once had was a huge step for me, I still had a lot of work to do.

Throughout my teenage years, I was drowning mentally, emotionally, spiritually, physically, relationally, and any other "ally" you can think of. I didn't know which way was up and which way was down. Picking up that book was like reaching for a hand that pulled me to the surface. It truly was the turn of events that I feel saved my life.

But that did not change the fact that I was still a choking wet mess once I was on the surface! Even though I wasn't drowning anymore, I was still very shaken up. I didn't know what I was doing. I still hadn't dealt with my past and had no idea what to do with my future. I was just there on the surface—alive, safe, and breathing.

I still had to figure out what comes next...

2

WHAT COMES NEXT

'd like to push the pause button on my story for a minute and admit something to you. Telling my story has been hard for me because of one very important thing—I don't find it unique. While this story might be unique to *me*, I do not find it unique to the world at all. In fact, I know you may have walked through similar or harder things.

A lot of families split up, and so many kids are growing up faster than they feel they are ready for. This story is more "normal" than abnormal in our generation. Beyond divorce, there are other traumas like natural disasters, death, abuse, suicide, drugs, illness, addictions, and difficult experiences that are common and familiar throughout the whole earth.

There is both public and personal tragedy in every person's life, and while we won't be able to stop all of these things, we do get to choose how we *deal* with tragic events once they've impacted us. We are responsible for deciding what comes next.

The white plate

I've had this analogy in my head for a while of a broken plate that I think might illustrate what I'm trying to say. At birth, we are a whole plate—perfect, white, and brand new. However, as we go through life, there are blows, both big and small, that begin to take their shot at the plate. Some are others' doings, some are our own, some are natural accidents that come from being a plate. Some hits leave little cracks and chips, while others leave long, deep fractures ready to split the plate in two. Once in awhile, there may be a fall that shatters the whole damn plate. What is left of our lives after such instances may be completely unrecognizable.

Once our 'plate' is injured, we have two options: We can spend the rest of our lives wishing we were never hurt, longing for the former days when we were young and innocent, or we can go about picking up the pieces.

I'm here to tell you that no matter what has happened to you in your life, no matter how broken you may think you are, healing is not only possible, it's probable. I'm here to teach you how to pick up these broken pieces and truly heal. I'm here to help you recognize where exactly the 'break' is in you so that you have an idea where to start. There are many different parts that make up the whole of you. Like a plate that shatters, we need to find and pick up each piece.

So what do we do? The remainder of this book will address just that. What do we do with our broken pieces? How do we get back up and still live a happy and healthy life? Part 3 will address all of these things in detail, but first, part 2...

PART 2
THE WORK

If you are anything like me, you are going to want to jump over this part as if it were a pack of hyenas nipping at your ass! I know it's scary. I know this part will be hard, but I will say that true freedom is on the other side. You will realize that real 'hard' is living a life without taking these 3 steps. You will come to love them. You will come to find solace in them time and time again, and you will rely heavily on the comfort they bring.

True happiness and a lot of fun are to be had only AFTER doing your work. If this part is skipped, your 'fun' will be external, short-lived, and empty. You will come back to the same life lessons again and again until you pass gracefully through these 3 stages. I promise every second you invest in doing this work will be worth its weight in gold.

Before any of us will truly be able to move on from certain tragedies, we will need to work through 3 important things: one, the truth, two, grief, and three, acceptance and forgiveness. Without these 3 things, there is no real moving on.

Part 2 of this book is, in part, named after a beautiful human named Byron Katie and her 'work' which has helped me recently.[8] I will admit I had not heard of her nor read any of her books when I was doing my 'work' though. This is the raw, disorderly, and organic way I was able to find acceptance and forgiveness.

Each of us will have work that is entirely unique to our situation. Yours will look different than mine, but I hope in sharing my story, it might help you find yours.

3
TRUTH

"And ye shall know the truth, and the truth shall make you free."

-John 8:32

Coming to know Christ was like coming up for air. He seemed to know me so intricately, without being startled by me. He met me on my level and took my hand in loving guidance.

As I started to trust Him more, I noticed Him nudging me to clean up my life, starting with my mind. Little by little, as I read and spent quiet time alone, it was as if there was this spiritual highlighter that would light up areas of my life that needed my attention. There was no shame or guilt, only a clear direction as to what to do next; each step bringing me peace and comfort as I tried it, even if I failed at my attempts.

I remember an idea coming into my mind to sit down with a pen and paper to filter through what was actually true and what was not about my past. It was at this time of my life that I realized not everything I was telling myself was true. It was a painful awakening that took courage to admit.

It was just me and my pen and notebook in my bedroom, but oh, how brave I needed to be to do that exercise! I realized that in my heartache, I clung to thoughts and ideas that were hurtful. In carrying them around, I made them my reality, whether or not they were true.

Without knowing what I was doing, I began an investigation on the thoughts in my own mind, trying to discern the lies from the truth. I asked myself, *"Did this actually happen?" and "What did I make it mean?"* This process of discovering the truth is not for the faint of heart. It meant I had to admit my own lies and the drama I had made of an already tough situation. It was hard work!

What is beautiful about sitting down and writing out the thoughts in your own brain is that when you step back and look at the situation and realize the truth, *the truth will set you free!* I learned from that exercise that there are **facts** and then there are **stories** about the facts. The facts are the truth and the stories are opinions.

While the facts cannot be changed, you absolutely get to decide what you make it mean for you. For instance, a person could forget your birthday, and you could attach very little meaning to that. In your mind, the 'story' could be that they forgot your birthday because people forget things, or your story could be that they don't love you, and they never loved you, and you are unlovable to all people forever and always! Do you see what I mean? Call it what you want, your own brain, or the adversary, either way, we can really get in a mess inside our minds. We can allow it to be filled with all sorts of lies.

On the other hand, if the story you're telling yourself about a certain event brings peace (even when the circumstances were awful), most likely the author of that story is love and truth, or *God.* God's stories bring comfort. God's stories will lift your aching soul and give you direction. God's stories can turn even the most painful facts into something beautiful. God's stories set us free because they are the truth.

Oh, how I wish I had that old notebook to read what I originally learned from this exercise! I'll admit I don't remember what I originally wrote, but what I can offer here is some truths I've learned from doing this exercise since.

What other people do is not about me.

Years ago, I went back and read one of my old journals. In it, I was talking about what my mom had done the day the ambulance came. I wrote the facts of what happened, and then I continued saying something like, "It hurts so bad that she doesn't care enough about me to want to see me graduate high school and grow up and get married..." I went on and on, but you get the point. I made it about me. *It wasn't about me!* I'll let you in on a little secret: *What other people do has little to do with you.* It doesn't. The truth is that my mom was sad, she had a broken heart, and she expressed her pain and pled for love in the way she knew how at the time. She was doing her best, given her circumstances. This leads me to my next truth:

People are human.

I didn't get this until years later, sitting in a therapist's office in Vegas.

The conversation with Him went something like this: "I feel like my parents should have _____, and I wish they would have _____ and _____. And I am this way because of all of these things..."

Do you want to know what he said to me? *"Everyone feels this way."* He said, "There comes a point in a person's life, usually about your age when the pedestal they put their parents on as a child usually starts to lower a bit until eventually, you are looking at them more realistically."

He went on to explain that *my parents were human,* and now that I was older, it was okay to expect humanness from them. I believed this lie that my parents were supposed to go through life and be superheroes and not have big issues and always be there for me. It wasn't realistic and it set me up for failure. Lowering my expectations of them has done me a great deal of service. Lowering my expectations of *all humans* has been such a nice relief. And no, this doesn't mean that you allow abuse or even that you need to stay in unhealthy relationships. You do what is right for you. It just means you aren't surprised when you realize others have flaws.

Something I like to do now when I meet other people and am CONVINCED they are PERFECT is to remind myself straight-up from the beginning that they aren't. I imagine that they probably make ugly faces when they poop, and they have bad breath in the morning. They probably yell when they're mad. Just like the best of the best and the worst of the worst, they would crack if put under enough pressure. People are human.

People "should" do whatever they are doing.

Stick with me on this one. Even my wording, "My parents *should* have _____." This statement is, in itself, a lie. Since we have this conscience of right and wrong, we believe that everyone else should do "right" all the time. (This might get pretty deep.) I realized through reading about God's plan for us that we were sent to earth to learn and grow. Oftentimes we do that through making mistakes. All those people "should do" is the best they can. The older I've gotten, the more I realize that *every single human is doing just that.* They, whoever 'they' might be, "should" do exactly what they're doing because that is what they need to do to grow on their own path.

I have an incredible friend who has helped me understand this concept. She is older than me and much wiser. I call her my Indian medicine woman friend. If you need more of a visual, she is the personality twin of the grandmother on Disney's Moana.[9] I once went to her very sad and upset about someone I love who was struggling with drug addiction. I told her the awful story of how he was not doing well and how worried I was.

She looked me right in the eyes and said, "I don't understand the problem."

For real.

I blinked and said, "Uh, did you not hear me? This person I love is addicted to drugs, and he isn't doing very well. What don't you understand?"

She then took a deep breath and said, "Okay, let me put it this way…You believe in God?"

"Yes," I said.

She then said, "What if before this person came to earth, he asked God for one thing, and that was to be able to help people overcome addiction. What if God said, "Okay, but you'll need to walk through it to understand it." And this person said, "Yes, I'll do anything."

She then leaned in close, looked me in my eyes, and said in a firm voice, *Who are you to take that from him?*

That one sentence sent a lightning bolt of truth through my spine, with the solid reminder that *I am not God.* I do not have to play God. I do not have to take it upon myself to decide who gets to experience what in this life. Trying to take away his agency was not my place. Forcing people to only make the "right" choices was never God's plan; learning and growing was; making mistakes and relying on a Savior was. And although it is painful, sometimes there is no other way.

God wishes for us to do good things, yes, but He will not force it. Instead, He goes before us, willing to transform these "mistakes" into a powerful force for good if we will have Him to be our God. The very thought of that brings me to my knees. What an amazing, kind, patient, and forgiving God He is.

Since that conversation with my friend, I have not worried about this person since. I have my heart wide open with love, and I am willing to do anything and everything if and when he wants help, but he is a grown man now, and I have no desire to give him a different life than whatever one he wants for himself. He is gaining the experiences that he is here to gain, and there is nothing wrong with him. I love him, and I trust that *his story is his story to write*. I know, without a doubt, that God and he together have all the power to turn these heartaches into his greatest blessings one day. This person "should" do what he is doing because that is how he will become who he will be.

It's not over yet.

Something else I learned was that *everything*, and I truly mean everything, will be okay in the end. God is that good. Whatever you have desired and whatever you have worked for will be restored to you, eventually. He has a plan to right every single wrong. Not one thing will go unnoticed or unattended. If we have Him to be our God, all heartaches will be healed eventually. All sins are given the opportunity to be made clean, and all injustices will be made perfectly just by the Creator of the universe and the Maker of us all. Any thought I might believe that something will not be okay or not turn out right when I have done all I can, is, in its very nature, a lie.

There is always good.

When we are experiencing something hard, we think that is all that it is. We fail to recognize all of the good that is happening alongside the struggle. This is something I still need to remind myself of, and it is my family who is teaching me the most about it right now.

Before sending this book to my publishers, I sent it out to my family. Since telling my story includes them, I wanted to hear their thoughts and feelings. One thing that was a resounding response from them was that "There was still so much good." And, "We're still a family." Middle Sis said, "Yes, it was hard, but the sun still came up every day. God blessed us. There was so much joy—not just at the end, but during it." She went on to talk about sunrises and sunsets, holidays, and family get-togethers. There was still so much good.

Looking back now, I can see that I failed to be a part of a lot of that good because I didn't want to see it. I didn't want to be a part of it. I didn't trust that the good would last and so I blocked it out as much as I could. What I wish I would have known is that every situation has interlaced with it both good and bad, light and darkness, happiness, and pain. There is no separating the two. Now I recognize they will both always be there.

Everything I'm dreaming of now and striving for will bring with it its own set of struggles. And every difficult experience will bring with it its own set of joys. The trick is to relax and embrace them both as they come. Let them coexist together. Embrace the fact that this is how life goes and focus my eyes on the good as often as I can.

I'm not alone.

The most common story I repeatedly told myself throughout this time of my life was that I had to figure my life out on my own. That thought hardened my heart. That thought kept me from going back home when I know my family would have loved to have me back. That thought isolated me, and led me to rely on substances rather than people who actually might have been able to help me.

The truth is I'm not, and never have been, alone. *I have always had what I needed, when I needed it.* I had a loving sister and loving friends who took me in until I graduated high school. I had an apartment willing to lease to me before I turned 18. I had friends and jobs. And whether I believed in Him or not, I had God.

There is a great big world full of people willing to help. I could have asked. When I did ask, I got the help I needed. If help didn't come in the way I expected, it was because there were lessons that I needed to learn. God knew I needed to grow and allowed me the space to do that. Still, I was never left alone.

I was not alone in another sense. When I was younger and more naive, I felt like I was the only one going through something difficult. What I didn't realize was that *we were all hurting.* Every member of my family was experiencing pain. I was not the only one. We all felt alone. We all felt abandoned and were numbing in our own way. While the details may be different, there is secret pain hidden behind the smiles of almost everyone I meet. Everyone on earth is dealing with something hard; everyone. Their hard might look different than my hard, but the emotions are the same.

If I could go back and tell my younger self one thing, it would be that every single person will have a similar experience. Every single person is going to have something that shakes them to the very core. Every single person is going to face the blows of life that will break them. Every single person is going to have to figure out how to pick up their broken pieces and put themselves back together. We are not alone. We are in this together.

If you feel alone right now, let me and this book be by your side. Let this community be by your side. Let all of us do this together. Remind yourself and repeat after me, "We are not alone."

And finally, because I'm willing to be vulnerable, I'm going to walk you through what I'm working through right now. (Cue live icon.) Before I wrote this book, I wrote a free intro book that I gave away to subscribers on my website. It included a little bit of what led up to me leaving my parents home and my dad saying, "We're done being a family," and "You'd better find a place to stay." Shortly after I wrote and released this little teaser, I was cleaning my house when my dad called. My dad hardly ever calls. Instantly, my heart sank. I'm terrified of hurting his feelings. (This book is giving me straight up hives trying to tell my story the best I can without hurting anyone.)

When I called my dad back, he was cheerful. His words coming out were happy, but I felt like, underneath all that, he was sad. I immediately decided in my mind that it was because he read what I wrote and was upset about it. So then I felt sad too, and nervous and uncomfortable. I ignored this book for days, convinced I shouldn't write it!

When I got over myself and got back to editing, I sat over the lines I wrote about my dad. I've tried to figure out how to not include them. I've tried to meditate and go back to that day. This is the question that I keep asking—*"Did Dad actually say that?"* If you are familiar with the work of Byron Katie[10], you know she's going to want you to ask this question twice. My initial response is, "Yes." I've heard it in my head for the last 17 years. And then I ask, "Did Dad actually say that or did my 15-year-old brain (who was very much in shock, mind you) take whatever was actually happening and make it mean that?" And then I'm stumped.

I was reminded of another Byron Katie quote: *"Who is more hurtful: the person who wronged you once, or you for reliving it over and over in your head?"*[11] And then I realized the truth: I'm the one that heard whatever I heard and made it mean that I was alone. Whatever my parents did or said that night (or any time, ever) was *over* right after the *exact moment it happened.* What was far worse than anything anyone has ever done to me, or any mistake I've ever made, was RELIVING IT over and over and over again in my very own head. *I am the hurtful one in the story of my own book.*

As I've sat here pondering, I'm realizing another revelatory truth: *I wanted to leave!* I had been wanting to move out for years, and that was not because of how awful my situation was, but because I knew it was going to be a part of my life. I knew it was going to happen before it did, and I wanted it. *It called me.* (Insert Moana song here![12]) My heart had been longing to go and figure out life on my own. I was ready. That event just opened the door for me. I was so used to resentment and so overcome with the situation that I didn't realize *it was a gift* until now, 17 years, 3 months, and 1-ish day later (I think, because math and I are not friends).

Instead of feeling resentment or anger or fear of what anyone thinks of me telling my story, I feel *gratitude. I feel so thankful to God and my parents for giving me the exact life I needed in order to become who I am.* I'm so thankful for the opportunity to write this book because writing it alone is healing parts of me that I was sure were already healed.

The truth is setting me free!

4

GRIEF

I feel like I could have finished the book after the last chapter because, in a nutshell, that is everything. But if you're like me, that isn't enough, especially during the heartache. The fact that it took me over 17 years to get there is proof I could have used help earlier.

So, what if you don't have this perspective yet? What if you don't want what you have at all? What if you have sorted through the truth, found the facts, demolished the stories, and the facts still plain suck? What if you are currently still crippled with resentment, fear, or grief? Then what?

Then you allow yourself to feel. I mean it. You've heard of the stages of grief—denial, anger, bargaining, depression, acceptance. Go through them—all of them. This isn't going to be pretty, easy, or orderly. Your grief will not flow through these stages in a proper sequence. In fact, you might not know where you are while you are there, so let it be messy. It is messy! Take as much time as you need without judging yourself. Be gentle with yourself as you feel. There is no telling exactly when and how these emotions will emerge, so give yourself grace as they do. Oftentimes they come in waves—ebbing and flowing as we are able to take them on.

I have a friend who went through years of deep heart-ache. During that time, she was so strong; like, abnormally strong. I watched her face her trials with insurmountable courage and bravery. Two years later, she came to me and said, "I don't get it. Things are finally calming down in my life. I feel like things are so much better than they have been in so long, so why am I crying now? Why do I have so much anxiety *now*?"

I sat and listened with compassion. What entered my heart as she spoke was this: Traumatic events are like a storm. When the storm is raging, we do our best to take cover, hold on tight, be strong, and wait for it to pass. During the storm, we live on adrenaline, are carried by angels, and have abnormal strength. It is after the storm has quieted, when we have a moment to breathe, that reality sinks in. It is here that grief often strikes us—a*fter the storm,* not during.

Anyone who has lost a loved one knows what I'm talking about. The shock of the death and funeral arrangements keep you so busy you usually can't process much. It is usually after everyone walks out the front door that grief slips quietly in through the back. It doesn't sound fair, but I believe it is far better to have a safe, quiet space to process. It's like an animal mother in nature who waits until she is safe and alone before she gives birth to her babies. Her body and soul know she needs to feel safe to experience the monumental transition. The timing of your emotions will probably emerge on an otherwise simple day where all circumstances might make you think you should feel happy.

For me, they come up when I am quiet. Because of this, I used to fill up my life with noise and busyness. Now I invite the quiet. When my babies go to bed, and my husband is away, I leave all electronics off and listen to my own heart, inviting it to tell me what I need to know. You'll be amazed at how even some of the yuckiest emotions are a gift and guide to joy.

When I got pregnant for the first time, I knew nothing about giving birth. Honestly, the thought terrified me. I avoided thinking about it because my body would tense up, and I would feel on the verge of an emotional break-down. I remember wishing there was a way for me to give birth without the actual act of pushing a child out of me! I couldn't think about it. I was in constant terror of the inev-itable outcome.

At about the halfway point of my first pregnancy, I knew I couldn't avoid it anymore. This baby wasn't going anywhere. She was going to have to come out somehow! One day, I surrendered. I realized that no one on earth could switch places with me and birth my baby for me. I had to do it myself, and if I had to do it, I wanted to feel every bit of it. It's hilarious to type this right now. I'm thinking, *"Wow, how did I come to such a dramatic conclusion?! Why not give birth and take the dang meds along with it?!"*

True to my nature, it was all or nothing, and I was all in. I wanted to face my fears. I wanted to know my own strength. I wanted to feel what it felt like to give birth to my child, unmedicated. I wanted to be awake and aware of every ounce of myself as I met her.

I started reading everything I could about how to stay calm during natural childbirth (because I assumed it would be as horrific as portrayed in the movies). What I learned was that my body was made for this.[13] I was made to give birth to a baby, and the whole experience could actually be very positive and beautiful. I became incredibly passion-ate about the idea, so much so that no one could talk me out of it. I guarded the entire experience as the protective mother I didn't know I was becoming.

I will tell you that absolutely nothing could have fully prepared me for what I felt, absolutely nothing. I have come to know that nothing of that magnitude can ever truly be understood before or even after. It is only ever truly known at the moment. When I was in labor, I was, however, wildly aware of two things: One, If I resisted and tensed up in fear, the contractions hurt worse, and two, if I relaxed and allowed the pain, it hurt less. *Resistance increased the pain.*

That lesson has stayed with me.

So, allow yourself to feel. Open your heart up and be willing to sit with whatever comes up. In her book *Love Warrior,* Glennon Melton says two things that have helped me: "What if pain - like love - is just a place brave people visit?" and, "Maybe instead of slamming the door on pain, I need to throw open the door wide and say, 'Come in. Sit down with me. And don't leave until you have taught me what I need to know.'"[14]

It's safe to say these quotes changed my life. I used to feel so guilty about feeling. I thought I was only supposed to feel certain emotions, and if I wasn't feeling the "good" ones, I was doing something wrong. So there was anger ,and then there was shame surrounding my anger, and then I was resisting that shame! NO WONDER I tried to numb that garbage. That's too much.

Now I know my emotions are my teachers. They are an indicator that some *thought* or some *thing* needs my attention. They are not bad. More importantly, I AM NOT BAD for having them. So, I practice allowing them. I *lean into it*, as they say. There is so much out there in the online world about this right now. Much of the advice focuses on sitting still and meditating to allow your emotions.

While I am falling in love with meditation, I will say that in the beginning, this was harder for me. Since I'm a person driven by being productive, sitting still to feel my emotions only added to the already excruciating practice of feeling the feelings in the first place. So what you'll find here are some other hands-on approaches that can help you process your emotions in healthy ways. Each emotion and situation have different approaches that work best, but I have a few go-to's if you need some help.

Anger is a fun one for me. When I'm really mad, I run. Anger is a secondary emotion. It's an outer layer protecting an inner layer. I don't spend a lot of time listening to what anger has to say mentally because I know anger is like the protective older brother who just wants to hit someone. Instead, I try to notice this emotion asap and redirect it to a healthier, although equally intense, activity. My goal: to allow the pent up tension to leave my body.

When I run as therapy, I leave my headphones at home, go outside (no matter the weather), and put on my sturdiest running shoes. With each stride hitting the pavement, I imagine stomping that crap out of my body. Do I look like a duck? Possibly. I don't know! But what I do know is that there's something about the combination of sweat, endorphins, and fresh air that works every time.

I will usually let loose in my head and say everything I want to say. Oftentimes I end up laughing over how funny my argument gets or cry when I realize what it was really about. Have you ever run-cried before? It's the best kind of cry. You need to run-cry at least once in your lifetime!

Anyway, when I get inside, I head straight to the shower. I visualize all the leftover emotional dust being washed down the drain. I imagine the water is a bright light filling me up with peace. I massage my shoulders and my scalp. I rub my feet. I breathe.

If you're going through a lot, do this often. Your job at this point is not to decide anything. You don't have to have any answers at all. In fact, the ideas you might come up with while you're still angry aren't usually the best. Your job right now is only to feel.

For me, I love to process anger with some intense movement and sweat. Think boxing, swimming, dancing, weightlifting. You get the point. I'm sure even yoga or a brisk walk would do. Just be intentional. Recognize the emotion you're feeling and give it a way out. Once I feel the emotion release, I feel better equipped to address the underlying cause.

My go-to for finding and acknowledging my other emotions? I almost always paint. And I'm not talking about the pretty pictures I want to show my mommy! I ugly paint, or draw, or color. If you looked around at the artwork in our house right now, you may not know whether I did it or my 5-year-old daughter brought it home from kindergarten! If it's cute and has some order to it, it's hers.

It doesn't matter what I use to do it. An ancient box of broken crayons? Even better. An envelope from the bill sitting next to me? Sure. What matters is that I sit still and try to color what I feel. That's it. I am amazed every time how good it feels. I go back to that place where I am like a kid again. I look at the colors, pick the one I'm drawn to, and then sit inside myself and notice. Where in my body is this feeling? Is it all up in my head like a firework freak show or is it a pit in my stomach that feels like a black hole? Where is the emotion? If I could give it a color, what would it be? What would it look like? And then I let loose. It evolves, and colors come up that remind me of certain people or things. I always learn about myself when I create art in this way. It is a revelatory experience.

The miracle about this process? You can work through garbage from your childhood trauma while your toddler thinks you are hanging out! You can't always drop your life and get sweaty, but anytime, anywhere, you can usually grab a sticky note and draw for two minutes. Don't have a pen and paper? Use your finger on your leg. I'm telling you it works. It pulls me into this meditative state that helps me acknowledge myself. Because honey, if you ever want to feel validated, you've gotta be the one to do it! Validation means less when it comes from outside of you anyway.

What you're really hungering for is your own self caring about you.

I love this art stuff so much I created a course and teach classes on it.[15] I got on a stage in front of way too many people and did a TEDx talk on it.[16] I'm telling you it's life-changing! You've got to find a way to feel your feelings.

If drawing or running isn't your jam, find something else. I also write letters, but not letters I actually send. I mean the uncut version of letters; the "What I would say if I could say ANYTHING" letters. I have a hilarious amount of those too.

Talk it out, move it out, lay on the floor, and cry it out. Find a therapist, find a friend. Do what you have to do, just let yourself feel whatever it is that you need to feel.

So if any of you are as overwhelmed as I was and in need of some help about how to go about this logistically, this is how it works for me: When I'm going through my day and feel some crap coming up, I decide then and there that I'll be putting my kiddos to bed early. I schedule the time to address the emotion. As dumb as that might sound, I need to be able to compartmentalize this in my life to function as a mom. After the kiddos are asleep, I turn off all electronics, silence my phone, sit, and breathe. Sometimes I pray. I practice being honest with nobody else but myself and God. And then I ask myself what I need.

Sometimes I end up talking out loud, sometimes I write, sometimes I sit in meditation, sometimes I color, sometimes I stick in my headphones, and dance like nobody's watching because for real, nobody is watching. I give myself the time and space to feel, however my body requests it. Am I weird? Probably. Does it work? Yes. So I'm willing to share it.

We will talk about this later in the book, but you already have the answers to healing within you. Your body, your spirit, they know what to do. We only get in our own way. So don't overthink this. Give yourself quiet time and some healthy options to choose from, and go from there. The better you get at this, the more quickly and painlessly you will process the harder times in your life. Feeling the crap will allow you to feel good more fully and more often.

The anger run? I haven't done that in years because I haven't needed it. Now I run for fun. I've learned that anger, for me, usually comes from stuffing my fears or sadness for too long, or has come from me not validating myself the way I needed to. Anger, bitterness, resentment- they're all emotions that don't come up as often for me anymore because, and this is the catch, *I am willing to feel them in the first place.*

We will continue talking about emotions throughout this book, but for now, I will tell you to stop resisting. The resisting hurts more than the actual emotion. I promise. Work through those stages of grief in your own way. Work through them until the sun can rise, and you aren't trembling. Work through them as they come because, naturally, after difficult experiences, they *will* come. Do the work. Be brave. You can do this.

Healthy grief vs. unhealthy grief

There are two types of grief: healthy grief and unhealthy grief. Healthy grief has laced within it an inner knowing of purpose and has hope that everything is going to be alright, even when you can't comprehend how. Healthy grief has compassion for self as one mourns and allows the space to feel. Even though *all* emotions might be felt, no matter how intense the pain, grieving is healthy when you have an inner knowing that this pain is creating space in you to become better. Healthy grief starts intense., then gradually spaces out and gets better as time goes on.

Unhealthy grief is different. Unhealthy grief feels overwhelmingly dark, is laced with harmful thoughts, and is present when faith and hope are gone. Unhealthy grief gets worse, not better, as time goes on. If you feel yourself losing your light or your mind is going to darker places, get help! Call someone who can help and tell them the honest truth about what you're experiencing.

Grieving is and should be a healthy process. Doug Manning says that "Grieving is as natural as crying when you are hurt, sleeping when you are tired, eating when you are hungry, or sneezing when your nose itches. It's nature's way of healing a broken heart. Don't let anyone take your grief away from you." He adds, "If you had major surgery, no one would pressure you to run a marathon the next week. Grief is a major wound. It does not heal overnight."[17]

Grief is actual work and may take the place of other work in your life for a time. Give it the space it needs to take its place; *knowing* that this is temporary; *knowing* that you will come out the other end better and stronger; *knowing* that a loving God is there by your side.

I'll end this chapter with a quote by C.S. Lewis because I think it perfectly describes what is happening when you have grief and why God allows the pain. He writes, "Imagine yourself as a living house. God comes in to rebuild that house. At first, perhaps, you can understand what He is doing. He is getting the drains right and stopping the leaks in the roof and so on; you knew that those jobs needed doing and so you are not surprised. But presently, He starts knocking the house about in a way that hurts abominably and does not seem to make any sense. What on earth is He up to? The explanation is that He is building quite a different house from the one you thought of- throwing out a new wing here, putting on an extra floor there, running up towers, making courtyards. You thought you were being made into a decent little cottage, but He is building a palace. He intends to come and live in it Himself."[18]

5

ACCEPTANCE AND FORGIVENESS

I f you continue on, doing the work of grief, you'll hit a point where you've processed enough, and really are wanting some closure. The sharp pain has turned into a dull ache, and you want to figure out how to move on already. I wish so badly someone could have taught me this back in the day because I stayed in this dull ache stage for years. I would say to myself, "*I want to forgive and move on, but how? How do you forgive when it still hurts? And if it still hurts, does that mean I haven't forgiven?*"

It helps to break this down.

Who are you needing to forgive? Someone else, yourself, an act of nature, God, life? It helps me to break it down and look at these scenarios individually.

Forgiving others

Let me start out by clarifying what forgiveness isn't:

- Forgiveness is not saying that what happened was right.
- Forgiveness is not saying that what happened was okay.
- Forgiveness does not mean you have to go back to an unhealthy relationship, or even spend time with

anyone who you do not want to spend time with. You don't. Let me repeat that in another way. *You absolutely can forgive with your entire heart and still choose to end a relationship.*

- Forgiveness does not mean you have forgotten everything. You'll probably remember (unless you're like my husband with a killer ability to forget negativity, God bless him).

- Forgiveness does not mean that you do nothing to fight for legal justice or protect others by notifying certain authorities. In fact, I need to pause on this one for a minute. If what has been done was illegal, if you or others have been abused in any way, *you have every right to say something.* You are not responsible for a single thing that happened, but you *can* tell the right people that it did in fact happen. Speaking up can help protect other people who interact with this person in the future. If nothing else good comes from this situation, your willingness to stand up for yourself and others will be made stronger. That is a blessing you'll appreciate forever.

And finally...

- Forgiveness is not about the other person. *Forgiveness has been and always will be a gift that you give yourself.* If it brings comfort or improves the strain in a relationship, then so be it. But it is not about them. The two people involved in forgiveness? You and God. It is a gift you give yourself by handing your pain, your hurt, your struggle over to God, *knowing* He knows what to do with it; *knowing* He knows how to make everything alright; *knowing* it will be alright in the end; *knowing* that you still deserve to have a good life and taking the opportunity every single day to still have it.

It is reclaiming the happiness that rightfully belongs to you and moving forward with the best damn life you can have. It is not sugar-coating what actually happened, or making it better than it was. It is simply *letting it be exactly what it was and being happy anyway.*

There is a quote by Oprah that has changed my life and my ability to forgive. She said, *"Forgiveness is giving up the hope that the past could have been any different."*[19] Forgiveness is *giving up the hope* that the past could have been any different! I read that 4 times over the first time I saw it, so stunned I needed a moment to process.

What was I still hoping for? And was the hope doing me any good? It was the first time I realized exactly what forgiveness was—acceptance. It's the final stage of grief!

Forgiveness is accepting that whatever happened in your past is done; not that it was right; not that you would have done it yourself. It's just allowing it to be the thing that happened, because friend, it already happened! There is no changing it. Resisting that it happened causes you more pain and stops you from moving forward.

Do you know how long this step took me? Eleven years! Eleven freaking years of wishing that my parents hadn't split. Eleven years of going to that happy place inside of my mind where we were all together like the old times. Eleven years of hoping and wasting my birthday candles and prayers, asking God if we could be together again, *resisting what was.* Eleven years of waking up dream after dream that I was in my childhood home, and everything was back to normal. Eleven years!

I'm telling you, I know the terror that comes over you when you realize you have to give this up. I know the resistance. I know that you feel like you're going to sink into a black hole and dissolve into sudden death. You're not. I know it feels sad to give up this type of hope, but your growth is stunted until you do.

Note: I'm not telling you to give up hope for the future. The future holds possibilities that only God knows. If you want to hope for some future change, by all means, hope is what carries us through. What I am telling you to do is stop wishing *the past* were different. It can't be different. *It has already been done.*

The sooner you can do this, the sooner you can move on. I wish I could tell you exactly when and how this happened for me. I can't. I know it was shortly after reading that quote that something sank in for me. I feel like I just woke up one day to reality. I looked around me and realized the greatness in my life that never would have happened had they not split. I found *gratitude* for the fact that everything happened the way that it happened. I realized that Mom and Dad had different paths, and I was happy things happened the way they did. Their lives are totally different now. They both chose what they wanted for themselves and who they wanted to be, and I'm happy for them. I realized that life is beautiful as it is!

I, personally, don't hope for them to get back together anymore. I only hope that they are becoming who they want to be, whatever that might look like for them. I now know that in constantly living in this unforeseen fantasy for the future, I am wasting the beauty of today. I now believe that sometimes the way life plays out for us is better than our own plan. I now know that seemingly ugly events can transform into something incredibly beautiful.

Forgetting

The final crucial step in forgiving others is this mystery called "forgetting". Have you ever heard the phrase *"Forgive and forget"* and thought to yourself, *"I can forgive, but how will I ever forget?"* Forgetting, in the common way we think of it, may not ever happen. You will probably remember.

Understanding forgiveness on an even deeper level clarified this concept for me.

Forgiveness is releasing a debt.

When others wrong us, we immediately think they owe us—owe us an apology, owe us an explanation, owe us by trying to make it right. We feel we are the victim, and they need to pay. Right? Truly forgiving is forgetting there is a debt owed. It's releasing the desire to have anything from them in return for what has been done.

When you think of the bank account between you and the doer of the deeds, you imagine their account to be in the green, not in the red. Does that make sense? This is the final step of letting go—forgetting. Any time you ever bring up the relationship between the two of you in your mind, you mentally choose to remember there is no debt.

I would have had a hard time doing this had I not been reading about a Savior; A man who came to earth, lived a perfect life, and then took upon himself all imperfection that He might be able to pardon others' sins if they would let Him. The more I learned about Him, the more I realized *there actually, literally, is no debt owed to me.* There never was. He has already paid the price for their sins, *all of them.*[20] No one will ever owe me anything. Do you know who they owe? Him; the perfect judge; the man who understands all. That is how much Christ loves you. He doesn't want you to have to wait until the doer of deeds is willing to make it right. He stands ready to heal you *now* if you let Him.

So this issue that's bothering you, this deed that was done wrong, remind yourself it is between those responsible and God. It always was and always will be. YOU ARE FREE. You are free to let it go, move on, smile, play, laugh, and become your best you because the Master of the Universe who has seen all and knows every detail of the mess will expect nothing but change and a new heart before He is willing to forgive them. And 'not one jot or tittle' will be swept away until the proper price is paid and all is fulfilled.[21]

Let me illustrate this with a story about my kiddos. They both got a pile of quarters from my mom for Easter in their Easter eggs. They carried these quarters around for weeks until one day, they actually wanted to use them. Of course, Bubba had forgotten his. Sister ended up giving him 8 of her quarters for him to ride rides at the mall because Sis is sweet like that.

They played and had so much fun together. When we got home, my son couldn't find his money anywhere, and Sis began to cry. I told her not to worry. I had 2 dollar bills I could give her. I gave her the money thinking all was well—knowing Bubs would pay me later when he found his money.

Now, I don't know if it was because the money wasn't in quarter form and she didn't quite understand it was the same thing, but she was still mad at him. It didn't matter how many times I explained, "*Sis, these two dollars will buy you exactly what you could get with 8 quarters, only they're lighter and easier to carry around! Mommy paid you. You are free to take your money and enjoy it. Bubba owes me now!*"

To her, that wasn't enough. In her mind, Bubba didn't pay her, and it threw off her little 6-year-old heart that night. She couldn't grasp it. I couldn't help but love her. I couldn't help but see myself in her. How many times have I failed to recognize that the debt has already been paid?

I am promised complete and total healing if I but forgive and believe in and follow this Christ. The scriptures talk of mansions in heaven for those who 'take up their cross and follow Him.'[22] The debt has been paid. How many times have I cried myself to sleep reliving some debt, without realizing that the thing I'm mourning the loss of is already sitting in the palm of my hand, available to use if I want it?

Have you seen the picture of the little girl being asked by Christ to give up her teddy bear?[23] In the picture, she's grasping her little bear saying, "But I love it, God." And

He is saying, "Just trust me." What she doesn't see is that behind Christ's back is a teddy bear twice the size, brand new and so much better with a big beautiful red scarf on it. He's asking her to give up her small and worn teddy bear in exchange for something better. In the circumstance of your broken heart, Christ is asking you to give up your resentment. Many of us cling to it, unwilling and afraid to let it go. If only we could see that in exchange, He's willing to replace the space in our heart with the gift of JOY.

Let him replace it. Permit Him to make the change.

Healing through meditation

The transition from resistance to acceptance is more powerful with prayer and meditation—specifically the meditation I'm about to share with you. I've been doing this meditation for years. I practice it with all sorts of negative emotions, but my favorite is making the change from resistance to forgiveness.

In this meditation, I usually set a time where I can be alone for a longer period of time. I have predetermined a time and place because this meditation is more sacred to me than the others. In it, I make sure to sit still and usually upright. I place my hands in front of me and rest them on my knees (or ankles if I'm sitting in criss-crossed).

I close my eyes and breathe. I imagine in my mind all of my negative thoughts traveling down my head, down my throat and neck, down my arms, and into my hands. I then imagine the dark feelings in my heart and gut and the rest of my body gathering up and flowing up to my arms, down and out into my hands.

At this point, I'll sometimes shift my hands to the sides and ball up the darkness. I do another scan to make sure the negativity is out of my body and floating in my hands, and then I call out (usually in my mind) to my Savior. I ask him to come and be with me.

It is not very long before light appears in my mind, and He kneels in front of me. Instinctively, He reaches out, and I offer the weight of my little world to Him. At this point, if there is anyone else involved that I am worried about or struggling with, I'll imagine handing this person over to the Savior.

I have no idea why, but to this day, all I've ever seen in this meditation is Him touching this ball and it all disappearing. He never carries it himself. Perhaps He doesn't need to. It's already recorded, and he's already carried the weight of it. But He always seems happy to take my black ball and knows exactly what to do. I don't know how He does it. All I know is that He does. And I am different inside when He does. Sometimes afterward, He will touch my cheek or the top of my head and fill my body with light until everything feels well and He leaves me. I usually sleep for a long time after that.

Now, I don't know if that is all too sacred to share with the world. Some might mock my little meditation, but if there is one person that it might help, I'm willing to share it. Feel free to try it. You might see something different than me. Roll with it. Each time and each experience has been unique to the situation, but usually, the pattern is the same. I ball up the darkness and offer it to the light.

Forgiving ourselves

Okay, so what if you are the one who has hurt you? What if you've made some terrible choices that you wish you could undo? Been there, done that too. We all have. Do you remember how Christ knows all? He's already seen what has been done, so there is no hiding it. Please remember that nothing is too far beyond his reach to forgive. *He's already paid the debt.* Do you know why He did? *Because He loves you.* He knows you're worth it, and He wants you to be forgiven. He's been cheering you on all along, preparing the way if you will be brave and willing to improve your life.

You may have heard before that Jesus Christ is our true healer. I spent years thinking that He either didn't have the power to heal me, that I was just that messed up, or that He had forgotten me somehow. What I didn't realize is that His healing hands were tied until I did my part. Forgiving others, forgiving myself, and making things right—these were all my part. But how? How do we do it? Forgiving others seems to be the easy part, but forgiving myself? That felt damn near impossible.

The things I've previously mentioned are all applicable here. Remember you are human and that humans aren't perfect. Remember that you "should have" done exactly what you did because that is exactly the life lesson you needed to learn in order to be here now. Remember that God can turn all our mistakes into something beautiful. He knows everything, including the details of your heart, why you do what you do, and that has a way to make right every wrong.

Do you remember that book I read? It taught me that change is possible. Just because I had done something in the past did not mean that I needed to keep doing it. So how do you forgive yourself when you mess up? Follow these 5 steps:

1. **Stop beating yourself up.**

   I mean it. It's not helping. I want you to think of one thing you have done that still comes up in your mind to haunt you. Do you have your thing? Good.

   Now, I want you to realize there are millions of people who have done the exact same thing you have; millions, if not more. That doesn't make it right. That doesn't make it okay, it just means you're not alone. We're humans and doing things we wished we didn't do is a part of being human. When we mess up, we tend to think we are the worst being on the planet. That's not true. Know that right now. You're not. You made a mistake. You aren't THE mistake. The fact that you are even reading this book, the fact that you feel bad about this thing, whatever it is, shows your heart. And you want to know what is even more important to God than actions? The desires of our hearts. He knows we are weak. He knows we're down here trying to figure this all out. He knows the use of our minds are limited and the control of our bodies takes an incredible amount of effort and time to master.

Know this: If you feel bad about something, use it. Let that emotion be a gentle teacher, guiding you to know what to do next. Let it say to you, *"Hey, we obviously care about this, let's work at it until we're better."* Do not allow it to cripple you, or demean your worth. You are God's child and you are loved.

It's helpful if you can do this with me: Close your eyes, take a deep breath, and repeat after me, "I am a good person. I love myself and _____ doesn't define me. " Repeat it till you believe it and then continue repeating it every day.

2. **Have hope in a better version of you.**

What's done is done. All you can do from here on out is take steps toward becoming a better person. Later in this book, I'll be going into detail about different aspects of our lives. You can improve each part, including wherever this mistake lies. There is hope. Hope is a thousand times more useful when you hope for things that you have the ability to work toward rather than hoping that something outside of you will change. Have hope that through Christ, you can become a better version of yourself.

3. **Do your best to "right" the wrong.**

What can you do to make this thing right? Sometimes there is nothing to do but move on already. Other times you might need to fix something the best you can. Did this mistake involve someone else? If so, approach them and apologize. Admit your wrongdoing. Be totally honest. Ask for their forgiveness and offer to make it right. Easier said than done, I know. Still, It's easier to face your fears, be vulnerable, and apologize for something you have done, than to spend time haunted by regret.

4. **Work on becoming better.**

The more you do to change your nature, the less time you will spend apologizing and trying to make amends. I know that trying to change sometimes super ingrained habits is not an easy task, but you can do this. You need to know that change is possible, and if you keep trying, you won't struggle with this thing forever. We could fill entire libraries full of books on how to change. So I'll keep it simple here, and share only the things that have helped me the most.

One, *get down to the root of the behavior*. There is a reason why we do what we do. Learning why and resolving the 'why' is powerful. I have never experienced lasting change by stuffing my true desires or feelings. Instead, I know I need to resolve them, so I feel differently and then practice acting differently until it's habitual.

Two, when practicing, think of the things you WILL DO, not what you WON'T DO. This works like magic! I can't emphasize its importance enough. Think about the healthy option you will do instead. Do not think, "I'm not going to criticize my spouse anymore." Instead, think, "I'm going to find 10 things I love about this person every day and tell them these things as often as I can." I'm telling you, this is the best way to change an ingrained habit. It's a small shift with powerful dividends.

And third, *don't give up until you've got it*. Every time you try to change something about yourself, it is going to be hard at first, kind of a mess in the middle, and really great at the end. That goes for whatever it is—lying, cheating, criticizing others, over-eating, over-drinking. That is how it almost always goes. So let it be hard, let it be a mess, and keep going until you've become a better person. When you mess up, try again. Like a child learning to ride his bike, know from the get-go YOU WILL FALL. It's not a big deal. Eventually, you'll start falling less often until one day you feel confident in the newly learned skill.

That analogy is coming up because just yesterday, I took my four-year-old son to the park to learn how to ride a bike without training wheels. He was terrified and crying. I reminded him that he was so brave.

I said, "Remember when you first started swimming? It was scary, and then you got really good at it, right? Now how do you feel when you swim?"

He said, "Happy and really, really brave."

I said, "Bike riding is the same Bubs! It's scary at first until you get good—then it's super awesome."

He smiled and said, "Okay."

I wish I could insert a video here because, after a few tries, he took off (thank you, Strider bike inventors[24]), and as he was pedaling with his might, he was chanting, "Keep trying, you'll get bet-ter!" (Thank you Daniel Tiger song writers[25])

So to you, I'll say "Change." However long it takes—give up this thing that hurts you and those around you. No matter how awkward or difficult at first, keep trying, you'll get better.

5. **Bury the hatchet on your past.**

Just be done with it. When it comes up in your mind, place your hand on your heart, close your eyes, and refer back to step one. This time saying, "I am a good person. I love myself. My past doesn't define me. I am free to be human. I'm choosing to let this go."

When you let this thing go, it will be a blessing, not only for you but for everyone around you. Burying the hatchet allows you to show up in this world as you truly are—an incredible human being.

Forgiving life, God, natural disasters, etc.

I was supposed to write this part of the chapter last night. Instead, I curled up in a ball on the couch, watched Eat, Pray, Love[26], and gorged on Thai Food and frozen mangoes (because I'm human too). I was too stressed-out, for no other reason than I'm burning my candle at both ends. I'm exhausted.

This morning, my daughter woke me up and wanted to watch Moana.[27] Again, I ignored writing. I just wanted to soak up a quiet moment snuggling her. I still felt too tired to work. Ironically, there is a part of the movie that I needed to see. It illustrated this section perfectly for me. Let's indulge…

Moana didn't know how to sail. She had just left her homeland in search of finding Maui. Late one night, at the beginning of her journey, she fell asleep. When she woke, she realized she was going in the wrong direction. She turned her boat around too fast and flipped it upside down. Knowing she couldn't flip it back over herself, she said, "Um, Ocean? A little help?" Immediately lightning struck, and a terrible storm began to brew, tossing her relentlessly through the ocean. She woke up on a beach, a hot mess with a wrecked boat, so mad she kicked and yelled at the ocean.

It wasn't until then did she realize she was on Maui's island. *She was exactly where she was wanting to go.*

I referred to life, God, and natural disasters separately. I do not know every detail as to why certain things happen, but I do believe that God is so intricately aware of the details that these three might be one and the same.

Here's what I think: Like Moana being tossed in the ruthless storm, we too are often tossed about in this life, with no one to blame but God. *We think "He's being mean" and "How could He forget me in my time of need?"* We wonder if we've been forgotten. We fear we have been led here to drown.

I know it's scary. I see you. I hear you. I only want to ask you what if this giant storm in your life is leading you exactly where you want to go? What if the storms you face, whether figurative or literal, are turning you into a person you could have never dreamed of?

God is not interested in you having an easy life if it means that you stay small and weak. He has plans for you to become bold and brave and strong and more beautiful than you already are. There is sometimes no other way.

There is a song by Calee Reed that says:

> *"Why did you lead me here to this uncharted sea?*
> *Did you bring me here just to drown me?"*

She then responds as if God is replying to her question, singing:

> *What if I didn't bring you here to drown you,*
> *but to cleanse you."*

> - Calee Reed, *Cleanse You*[28]

So let it cleanse you. Let it lead you to where you are going. I believe there are times when we are being tossed about, and the lesson is to learn to sail to get to where we want to go. Sometimes we are meant to take control and do something about our mess. Other times, I believe we are meant to hang on, try not to swallow too much water, and wait for the storm to pass. Your heart will tell you which storm you are in. If you're in the second, know right now that this is not an accident. The God of the universe, your Father, knows you are in that storm and has every intention of it guiding you to where you were meant to be.

To cleanse is to make free of dirt, foreign matter, pollution, etc. I think it often takes a difficult experience for us to turn off the tv, put our phones down, and be still for the unnecessary dust to fall away. This is especially true when a loved one passes away. Those who have been called to go through this grief are hyper-aware of all of the things that don't matter as they mourn. They have been given the gift of cleansing. If their pain lasts, it stands as a reminder of what is truly important.

I loved the part in *Eat, Pray, Love,* where she realizes she's in trouble and needs help. She prayed for the first time out loud and said it was such a foreign concept to her that she almost began with "I'm a big fan of your work." She prayed anyway, from the depths of her heart. She expressed the trouble she was in and said, "I need your help. Please, God, tell me what to do, and I'll do it."[29]

Many of us, in our time of need, no matter how stubborn or non-religious previously, will turn our thoughts to a higher power. It is here that we become aware that the problem is bigger than us. We are humbled, and we connect with the heavens. Some of my most sacred moments in life were born in struggle.

In her book *Love Warrior,* Glennon Doyle writes, *"You have been offered the gift of crisis. As Kathleen Norris reminds us. The Greek root of the word crisis is "to sift", as in, to shake out the excesses and leave only what's important. That's what crises do. They shake things up until we are forced to hold on to only what matters most. The rest falls away."*[30]

You will be left with the golden nuggets at the end of this crisis. Without all of the excesses clouding it, you will value the jewels in your life more than ever before.

So how do you forgive? There is simply no need to forgive when you recognize what you have been handed was *a gift* in the first place. So close your eyes, trust that there is a purpose, and breathe Him in. I believe one day the sun will rise, and you will look around and realize you are exactly where you wanted to be.

The last thing I want to mention about forgiveness is that when I was doing my best to forgive, I remember wishing for a sign that I had forgiven the proper way. The sign I was looking for was for the memory and the hurt to be gone. Forgive and forget, right? Isn't that what they say to do? This confused me. I didn't think I had forgiven because I still remembered what happened. When I spent time remembering what happened, it still hurt.

Instead of thinking of forgiveness as a one-time event, for me, forgiveness has been a process, and my emotions have had layers. One at a time, certain aspects will surface. Each layer will have to be dealt with in its own time.

Do I believe that one day you will have worked through all of these pieces, and your lessons will be complete? Yes. Do I believe that you can get to a place where you are entirely free of pain, and instead, in its place, you'll feel full of gratitude and love? ABSOLUTELY YES!

Do I believe you can rush through this process? No. I'm sorry, I don't. I believe you can have an open and willing heart, but sometimes life will have lessons for you, and there is no way to work through it until you're there. I believe no pain is wasted. There is a purpose to your pain, and one day everything will be okay and make sense.

There is a story I heard years ago. I cannot recall where I heard it. It impacted me enough to carry the lesson through-out my life, and I think it's worth sharing.

In this story, there was a boy that had a strenuous rela-tionship with his father. He had been praying to understand where his father was coming from. He wanted to forgive.

He wanted to understand. He prayed and prayed with what were to him *countless* unanswered prayers. To him, it felt as if the heavens were closed. He didn't understand why heaven could be so silent for so long while he was pleading for such a worthy cause. It wasn't until He was a full-grown man that an answer came.

One ordinary day, standing in his living room surrounded by his own young children, feeling all of the emotions of a tender and vulnerable parent, his answer came. It was then, and only then, that he was prepared to receive it. God whispered into his heart what he needed to know, and he wept. Life had to carry him to that place where he would not only understand with his mind but would grasp all he needed to know with his heart. He needed to be a father himself. God heard every prayer. The boy had not been forgotten.[31]

The story reminds me that sometimes we cannot rush healing to the extent we want it yet. Sometimes time has to pass for us to fully comprehend all that we need to know. *Sometimes life is the answer.* Sometimes our experiences carry with it the key to our healing.

Knowing that complete and total forgiveness may take time, here is what I do: I don't worry about it! I deal with emotions as they come. When something surfaces that is bothering me, I know it's knocking on my heart because it's time to address it. I consider it a blessing. So, again, I focus on the emotion that is present. I do my work to deal with what I'm feeling as soon as possible, and then *I continue living my life as happy as possible.* Forgiveness is moving on with your life with joy in your heart.

PART 3
THE JOY

This morning I woke up at 3:30 am. I haven't been feeling well and all I want to do is work on this book! So I did a little bit of stretching, drank my lime water, and started to pray. In the middle of my prayer, I had a super random thought, albeit crystal clear, enter into my mind: "2 Nephi 2:25." Now, I'm not a scripture scholar. I don't have scriptures memorized, so I had no idea what that one said, but the reference continued to repeat in my mind throughout my prayer until finally, I stopped to look it up.

Here is what it said: *"Adam fell that men might be; and men are, that they might have joy."*[32]

Adam, as in Adam & Eve, *fell* in order to experience *joy*. I don't find that ironic as I sit here to write this chapter. God wanted to remind me of all we've been talking about—*The Pain* in part one and *The Work* in part two have been faithfully leading us to the final part in our learning cycle: *The JOY*. The "falls" in each of our own lives were given to us in order for us to fully experience joy. The harder the fall, the greater the joy IF we pick ourselves back up and overcome it.

Throughout the remainder of this book, we will be talking about picking up the pieces from our individual falls. Each piece will be a new discovery of who you are and what you might want for your life. Each new chapter will bring a certain part of you into the spotlight. It is my hope that you look at each piece as if you've never seen it before. Get to know yourself as if you are trying to get to know a new friend. Fall in love with new possibilities for your life that are yours for the taking. It is my hope that this book can be a new beginning for you, where you are given the opportunity to take a fresh look at your life and decide what you want.

Let me remind you, your life is for *you* to choose and no one else. I will be sharing my experiences of finding myself, but that does not mean that your story will look like mine, nor should it unless it feels right for you. Let yourself find you. Let yourself continue to find you over and over and over throughout your life.

The remainder of this book can be read in order, but I hope that after a while, you will feel free to refer to individual sections again and again as you dive deeper into each piece and add your own pieces. I relate this idea to creating a painting. I am an artist, and I like to paint big pieces of art. There is something about getting my whole body into the movement as I paint. But there is one challenge to painting big. When I am standing up close to the canvas, especially when I am working on a more detailed portion, I get lost! Literally, my eyes can't find their way.

I just finished a giant painting of Christ.[33] I will tell you that when I was working on His huge beard, I had no idea where I was at times. To find my way again, I would have to step back, take in the painting as a whole, and then I could see where I was going. Our lives are big. There are so many aspects and so many details. We get lost and forget what we are working on and why we are working on it.

Part 3 of this book is meant to be "the stepping back". This is the opportunity for you to take in everything as a whole so that you can zoom in to whatever area you would like to work on. I find it important to add that implementing Part 2:The Work may have felt more like an exhaustive sprint. Part 3: The JOY should feel more like a long, enjoyable walk.

The cycles of joy happen as you learn and overcome your cycles of pain. This is an ebb and flow, a gradual rise of the tide. Slow down, pace yourself, and give yourself time with each part, growing as you go. Start small. Little victories accomplished consistently will equate to bigger wins than you can imagine. As you grow and mature, you will notice each new piece taking on greater heights. Keep moving, keep spiraling upward, keep finding the joy.

6

PICKING UP THE PIECES

Giving myself the time to acknowledge my pain, find truth, grieve properly, and forgive, gave me a sense of peace that put me back in the driver's seat of my own life. Now that I feel I have some sort of say, I can go about picking up my pieces.

Do you remember earlier when I made the analogy of the broken plate? When a plate is broken, the sooner you can accept that it happened and forgive whatever broke it, the sooner you can go about cleaning up. If you haven't done your work emotionally and skip straight to the cleanup, this part will be miserable. You'll be filled with bitterness, and all sorts of obscenities will blare in between your ears as you go!

If you have done your work, this part will look more like a Saturday morning cleaning sesh with music blasting, your top knot a-swinging, and your broom acting as Beyonce's real-life microphone. Ya feel me?!

Forgiveness doesn't change the fact that the plate is on the floor, it only frees up very unnecessary hurt so that you can go about the clean up with joy. For me, this is the fun part. This is where we get to discover ourselves and *find out which of those pieces we actually want back.* This is where we get to join hands with our Creator and make something of our lives that we may have never previously dreamed of.

So, can I tell you about the moment I decided to write this book? I am a Therapeutic Art Life Coach, so I teach people how to use creativity as a means of processing emotions and healing. The entire conception of this book came about one day during training for that certification.[34] The instructor was talking about how we need to start seeing ourselves as a *whole person* and began breaking down the *parts* of this *whole*. After this 8 min instructional video, I sat in quiet reflection. For the next few hours, information flooded my mind. It was as if the ceiling broke on the barrier between me and the heavens and revelation came pouring in!

I thought about how when we get hurt, we tend to only see what we are struggling with, and that one thing consumes us. When I was young and my parents split, that was all I could see. I couldn't see my health, my talents, my other relationships, or any other part of me. I couldn't see the good in the other 90% of my life. When that one piece broke, I let all of me break.

I then began thinking of my own healing and how one by one, I have picked up these aspects of myself and put them back together again. It was as if in an instant, the fog had lifted, and I knew exactly how healing had come in certain parts of my life. I could also see clearly where I was still broken and knew exactly what I needed to do to put myself together.

As she spoke and listed a few things, my mind expanded and realized that there was more than she was willing to say. I sat and began to make my own list of things that make up who I am. I still look at and use this list. This list is a reminder to me that I am more than my mistakes. I am more than my body. I am more than whatever is on my mind. There is more to all of us. As we step back and take in everything as a *whole*, we can grow in ways we couldn't before.

The list I created that day after class is the one I'll be sharing with you, and I'll spend the remainder of this book referring to it. These are the parts that I believe make up who we are:

1. **Our Personal Space:** How we keep our homes, work environment, belongings, etc., and also includes the physical places we choose to be in.
2. **Our Physical Bodies:** The tangible parts of us.
3. **Our Spiritual Bodies:** The more refined, eternal matter that joins with our physical bodies.
4. **Our Mind:** The thoughts we choose to think.
5. **Our Voice:** How we express ourselves in this world through speaking, writing, art, what we wear, etc.
6. **Our Heart:** The centerpiece of our emotions, how we feel, and connect with ourselves, Deity, and the world around us.
7. **Our Intuition:** That "knowing" feeling inside of us.
8. **Our Sexuality:** How we experience ourselves with sex and sexual desire.
9. **Our Relationships:** How we relate to and connect with other people.
10. **Our Talents:** What we are drawn to or naturally good at, and how we use these things to make the world a better place.

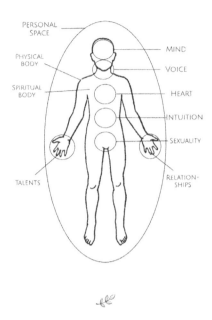

When my son gets hurt and comes to me crying, I comfort him, kiss his cheeks, help him breathe, and then ask, "Where are you hurt?" If he's still crying, I'll point to his knees or his toes and ask, "Does it hurt here or here?" I love seeing the shift in him as he goes within himself to feel where it is.

There is a change that happens inside all of us when we take our eyes off of what happened and who did it, to where it hurts, and what we can do about it. So to you, I would ask, "Where does it hurt? Where are your wounds? And where are you longing for a change?"

It takes insurmountable courage to truly look at yourself and get to know yourself on a deeper level. As we spend the remainder of this book working through each "piece", please remember that perfection is an illusion. I do not hope for perfection in any area of my life. What I hope for is awareness—awareness of where I am at, and where I am going. And then, I do my best to find joy in the journey of growth.

It's important to remember that certain life experiences don't necessarily mean one part will be "broken". I have four siblings and two unique parents. We all lived in the same home and had similar experiences together. Although we were in the same place, each of us felt very differently and struggled with different things. Like multiple people in the same car during an accident, we each walked away with unique wounds.

True compassion is recognizing that we are individuals with unique personalities and differences. Acknowledging that will give you the space you need to get to know yourself deeply, on a level never known before. While there may be others who have had similar experiences, your life is unique to you. The most compassionate thing you can do is look at yourself as if no one else exists.

God sees us this way—one by one. If you join hands with Him, He will nurse you back to health with such tailored precision that even you will not be able to comprehend it. You are His creation. He knows every detail of what your life has been like, and He knows exactly what to do.

I hope that as you read, you become aware of just how much good you do. I hope you will see the power you have to open yourself and your life up to finding joy in every part of you. *You truly have the right and the power to experience happiness in all of these areas.*

Also, as we dive into each of these areas in the coming chapters, you will notice that they overlap. Because you are a whole being, each piece relates to, connects, and affects the others. Like a spider web, when you pull on one end, everything shifts. Because of this, I don't concern myself with where to start. As the saying says, "A rising tide lifts all boats."[35] When you begin the healing process, no matter where you begin, *healing will overflow into other areas.*

Keep your eyes peeled and your heart open to whatever stands out to you in the coming chapters. Notice what pulls at you. Notice what gives you butterflies. And please,

please let yourself dream again! Whatever condition you find yourself in, no matter how destitute, it says nothing about your future. Your future is filled with endless, glorious possibilities!

This is the part where you get to decide again. This is the part where magic can fill your life. This is the part where you get to become YOU again—only a better you than you have ever dared to imagine.

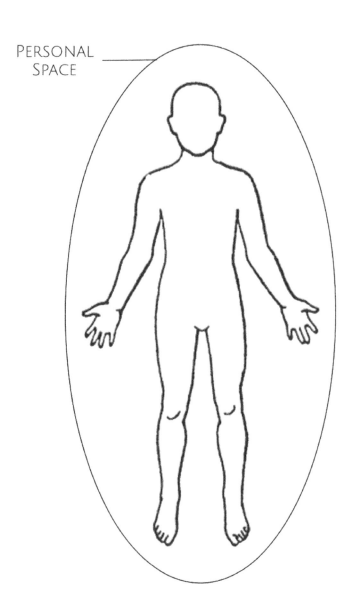

PERSONAL
SPACE

7

PERSONAL SPACE

Once you have looked at and properly dealt with some of your past, it's time to start moving on toward creating a better experience in the present and dreaming for a better life ahead of you. I'm beginning with this chapter on personal space because there is a magic that happens as you pick up your belongings. It brings clarity and space to breathe. It will open the doors for healing in all other areas of your life.

For many of us, after tragedy or heartache, we can't even fathom where to begin to start feeling better. The idea of tackling PTSD or emotional trauma seems like a giant mountain impossible to climb. May I suggest a better place to start?

Clean your room.

For real.

I know it sounds crazy, and I'm risking credibility on a book about healing by putting this up-front. But I'm serious. Clean your room. Your things are a continuation of you, so altering their condition alters you. Cleaning up your personal belongings has the power to calm your mental and emotional state in a way that other things can't.

Throughout the next chapters of this book, you will need a sacred space to sit in regularly that will allow you the peace and quiet you need to think. So starting here is the perfect place to set you up for success later on. Cleaning your room will give you a visual reminder that messy things can be renewed. Let this begin a ripple effect that will move to all other areas in your life.

As I write this book, I am 32 years old. I have moved 30 times since I was 15! I haven't always had control over whether or not those moves happened, but I will tell you that every single time I moved, I deep-cleaned my new space, organized my things, and created order to my confusion. This is one thing I can do.

If you are actually sitting in your room right now, I want you to look around. Don't be 'judgy' or hard on yourself, only admire it as if you were viewing the space for the first time. (If you're not in your room, I want you to look around at where you are at or imagine your personal spaces.) How is it? What do you love? What do you not love? What is the general feeling in your personal space?

There is no wrong answer here. Things get cluttered, and rooms get messy for all of us. It's okay if that is how it is right now. I only want you to recognize how it is. Bring awareness to the space around you.

Again, self-reflection takes courage. We'll be self-reflecting on much bigger and more important things later, so take time here to practice being gentle as you look around at your things. Take the day and notice the condition of your belongings. Ask yourself this question: "Is this how I want my personal space to be?" You don't have to begin frantically cleaning. In fact, for a minute, please don't! Only notice.

Everything around us is a symbol. Your personal space is a reflection of how you are doing. When our lives are filled with stress and chaos, our homes and things tend to get stressful and chaotic too. If this is how it is, take heart and thank yourself for all the incredible things you have been doing. Notice that you've been busy, or tired, or mourning, or whatever, and let it be okay that things got this way. All things can improve. Your environment can be renewed.

Once you feel ready and have a little time to roll up your sleeves to do some work, I want you to start creating a sacred place for yourself. I like to begin with my bedroom, but you can start anywhere.

Do all the things you need to do—take out the trash, pick things up off the floor, donate, sell or throw out the junk you don't use, vacuum, wipe down surfaces, change your sheets, and find a home for all the things you use and love. This can take as long as you want it to, but start today and don't stop until at least your room is clean.

After this, I want you to wake up every morning, and if NOTHING else, I want you to make your bed and keep things picked up in your room. Make this your baseline. You see, I want you to know that even if WWIII is happening outside the walls of your room, you have this oasis to come into. You don't have control over a lot of things in life. Take ownership of this space, however big or small. If you share a room, do what you can to create your space and have it be peaceful. Every morning when you wake up and every night when you come home I want you to see that what once may have been messy is now clean. I want it to stand as a reminder to you that *things can change,* and *you have the power to make these changes.*

Once your room is clean, feel free to continue to what-ever other belongings you have. How is the rest of your home? Your car? Your purse or backpack? Your workspace? Is it how you want it to be? If not, make the shift.

As you begin to turn the table on your environment and embark on this upward spiral, you will notice yourself caring more about your personal space. *You'll want it to feel like you.* Let this practice of caring for your things become almost ritualistic; a time to discover yourself and all your likes and dislikes. Put on music you love. Light incense or a candle or diffuse oils. Choose scents that you are drawn to. Notice what lights you up about your belongings. What colors do you love? What possessions do you love? Move those things front and center. Fill your room and your space with things that Marie Kondo says, "spark joy".[36]

As you do this, you'll get to know your personal style (not your mom's style or what is popular on Pinterest, YOUR STYLE). You'll get to know yourself as if you're getting to know a new friend. We are constantly changing. Just as you need to continue to get to know a spouse or your children, you need to continue to get to know yourself. As life changes, *you* change. Your personal environment should change and evolve with you. Work to embrace those things that are resonating with you at the moment. This is something small you can do for yourself; an act of self-love.

As you continue to do this, you might notice yourself being more careful about what you buy or bring into your house. You'll want to guard it as if it were special because that is exactly what your personal space will become to you—special.

Healing happens not only as we nurture ourselves, but as we nurture something outside of ourselves. Your personal belongings are a great place to start. Keep what you love and learn to let go of the things that no longer serve you. You will feel lighter and happier every time you choose to release parts of your past that served you well at the time and are now meant to move on.

Let me also say that you don't need to spend any money to improve your personal environment. Start with what you have and make the best of it. You don't need expensive things. You don't need to have a huge house. You absolutely do not need it to be perfect!

In fact, right now as I'm typing this, I am sitting in our 5th wheel trailer, which is actually our home. My husband and I and our two kids have been living here for almost two summers while we are building a new house! Our life is not perfect. Our personal space is not always perfect. I'm sitting on my bed (which is also my office), and literally, if I lied down sideways, I could touch my feet on one wall and my hands on the other wall! Our current personal space is not big, but it is taken care of, organized, and, in my opinion, super pretty. We fixed it up to look like the fresh white home we are building, and it *feels like us*. My point? It does not matter how new or expensive or big your things are, taking care of what you have will give you a sense of serenity and gratitude for what you *do* have.

Side note: Obsessively cleaning shouldn't be an escape from your emotions or an unhealthy means to be 'in control'. Remind yourself that you own your things, and they should not own you. Your home will not be perfect all the time. Dirty laundry will sit in a hamper, dishes will touch the sink, and dust will accumulate. Perfection isn't important. What is important is to be aware of what is going on around you and to be intentional with it as often as possible.

Another part of considering your personal space is becoming aware of the places you frequent. Where are you spending your time? Do you spend your personal time at bars and clubs, or do you frequent the yoga mat at your local gym? What movies do you go to? What is your work environment like? And what spaces do you choose to be in most often? Is it where you want to be? Or are there changes that you'd like to make?

Turning my life around meant that I had to start switching up where I was spending my time. I went dancing at clubs less and stopped going to so many parties. I got a gym membership and traded my time that was once spent in environments that weakened me for places that made me feel strong.

(If you're interested in diving deeper into self-discovery while you read these chapters, feel free to download a free Becoming Whole journal on www.heatherfalter.com. In it, you can fill in each chapter's questions as you go along.

For now, I will leave you with one last question: If you did one thing today to improve your personal space, what would it be? Now go and do that thing and embrace the fact that you have already begun healing.

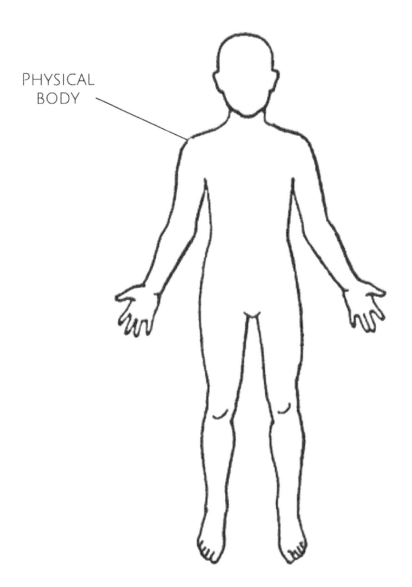

PHYSICAL
BODY

8

PHYSICAL BODY

If you have walked through hell, you were not alone. Your body has walked through it with you. Your body is a constant in your life; your hands, your feet, your skin, your hair. They were there. They went through that too. They felt everything that you did; the Cortisol, adrenaline, lack of sleep, all of it. You have probably noticed certain stresses visibly take their toll on your body.

We truly go through a lot. Even if you've never been through anything too intense, your body is under stress every day from living life. There are toxins, viruses, bacteria, and heavy metals and crap in our food that shouldn't be there. It is no wonder that when life gets extra hard, physical symptoms show up with it. Your body was most likely already stretched to its limits.

All of our bodies could use some extra lovin'. They are at our mercy. They rely on us to learn about them and care for them. Fortunately, most of us are willing to care for them, we only need the right information. There is a lot of confusion as to what is truly healthy for us. Most people give a diet or exercise regimen their 'all' with no real improvement in their health. I hope I can help shed some light on why you aren't healing.

I wanted to address our bodies near the beginning of PART 3 because for many of us, this is what we think of when we think of ourselves. Our physical bodies receive the most attention because they are tangible. We can see them, hear them, smell them, touch them. This is super helpful when it comes to healing because when outside forces hurt our bodies, we can often see it. We get help faster when we can see the wound. That's unfortunate, but it's true.

When we break an arm or leg or split open a lip and need stitches we don't hesitate. We go to the doctor and get help. Nobody judges us for getting help in these situations because they can see it too. We are comfortable in these moments. I once needed surgery after I fell and broke my arm snowboarding. It was a no-brainer. I could see with my eyes that it was in the shape of an "S" and I got help. It is in times like these that I am so glad that we have come as far as we have in medicine. I'm so grateful for doctors, surgeons, and anesthesiologists!

But what if your body is suffering and the answers don't quite seem so simple? What if what ails you is more chronic and long-lasting? What if you have developed an illness and struggled with it for years or even decades without any clear answer of how to heal? What if other people can't see it, and you aren't validated in your pain? Then what?

I was 20 years old the first time a doctor sat me down, concerned about my health. I was young, fit, happy, and training for a marathon. I hadn't been to the doctor in years and wouldn't have been there had I not had to get a check-up for a church mission that would send me out of the country.

I hadn't ever been to a doctor (or dentist for that matter) without a huge thumbs-up, and an "everything looks perfect". When this doc came back from doing blood work, she looked worried and said, "I'm concerned. Your cholesterol is extremely high for your age." She continued talking about my heart and what that might mean for my future if I didn't get it under control.

She then asked this question, "What are you eating?" I kid you not, that was the first time anyone in my life had ever asked me that question without wanting to order what I was having on the menu! I fumbled for words because the only thing coming to me was, "*Uhhh, EVERYTHING. Literally, everything ma'am. Everything.*"

I was born weighing only 5 pounds with a huge appetite and I swear to you, it had never let up. "Full" was not a feeling that happened to me. I was ALWAYS HUNGRY. I had no idea what food was good for what, beyond what tasted good. I was small so there was never any concern for me. Most everyone seemed to consider it a good thing that I ate so much and I liked to help them feel better about themselves by doing it. I single-handedly ate many tables full of leftovers and can still hear the common phrase spoken almost every evening in our house, "Don't clear the table, Heather is still eating!"

This was the first time I was told by someone in authority that I needed to stop eating certain things if I wanted to live a long life. I was disheartened, to say the least. My health issues did not stop there. Months later I had a seizure that I kept secret to stay on my mission. I battled years of extreme fatigue (only pretending I wasn't fatigued). I struggled with acne, hair loss, anxiety, depression, insomnia, and a whole slew of more personal issues I won't bore you with here.

It wasn't until I was pregnant with my first child 5 years later that I was diagnosed with hypothyroidism. After learning the symptoms I laughed and said, "Oh, that explains so much of my life!" I thought I had figured it all out and I was so relieved to have an answer that I didn't mind being on medication. I'll be honest, there wasn't a lot of physical difference on or off of the medication that I could tell, but there was something very comforting about the doctor validating what I was going through.

I did, however, wonder if the medication was actually helping me. I hated the idea of needing a pill to be "healthy". I remember asking my doctor over and over, "Is there anything I can do to heal my thyroid through foods?" I could tell that was such a foreign concept to him. He didn't know how to answer. He just shrugged his shoulders and said, "You could try!" (Without any guidance as to what to "try".) I could tell he was holding back a smile—like that was such a laughable concept! Still, I tried.

I call this my 'experimental phase' where I tried just about every fad diet and 30-day program there was out there. My diet was also full of weird concoctions like homemade sauerkraut and shots of apple cider vinegar before and after meals. No success. My thyroid grew worse. Each time I went to doctors, my medication was increased. Between my first and second child, they had tripled my dose. My heart was aching for answers.

After my second child was born, I tried one particular diet that did seem to help. I saw progress in a lot of areas, and it sparked hope in me that what I was eating *could* improve my health (go figure!) The only problem was that this diet was incredibly strict, even for me. I wondered how on earth I could keep something like that up long term. I was determined though, and I kept it going the best I could for almost two years. My thyroid levels were improving, but I was also becoming very aware of how hard it was to process some of my old foods if I slipped up.

A few years later, I woke up feeling funny. I like to wake up early, and this particular morning I could tell something wasn't right. I was walking around, but I didn't feel like I was entirely in my body. I felt like I was floating above it, and it totally weirded me out. I knew I needed to lay back down. I was in my living room, and as soon as I laid on the couch, my eyes rolled into the back of my head, and my body began convulsing. The same thing happened that happened on my mission.

Two weeks later, I found myself sitting in a specialist's office going over my game plan of an MRI and possible radiation treatments and surgery. He was entirely sure he was dealing with a pituitary tumor. My doctor wisely ran a full blood panel with his testing to make sure his diagnosis was correct. Waiting for those results were some of the longest few days of my life...

When the results came back, we learned that my pituitary was fine, and I was diagnosed with hypoglycemia instead. It turns out my blood sugar levels were sitting at a 54 in his office, and that was on a really good day for me. I didn't quite know what that meant. I felt fine so, I assumed it was not a big deal. The specialist had to wake me up by saying, "*You should not be able to sit here and chat normally at this level. You should be passed out on the floor.*" He gave me a 90% chance of having type two diabetes in the coming years and tried to stress to me how important it was that I make a "solid lifestyle change."

A lifestyle change. For real. Anyone who knew me by this point only knew me as someone entirely disciplined with healthy eating and exercise. The lifestyle change he was asking for was very similar to the way I had been eating for years. In fact, he brought up the diet I was on and said I needed to make sure I followed it 100 percent. I was glad to have the direction to do something that I was already good at! Still, I was confused. Why was this happening? If that were the correct diet for me, why wasn't I healthier? I was already eating that way. Something wasn't right.

My already strict diet turned more strict. He increased my fat intake, lowered my carbohydrates even more, restricted certain fruits and veggies, and put me on an even more intense exercise regimen. I can honestly say that it did help in the beginning, but slowly it lost its great effects. I was getting more tired and my levels were getting worse with each visit. My doctor's suggestions were not working...

I finally came to the conclusion that I needed help beyond any mortal man or scientific research. What I was told to do wasn't sustainable long term. I felt great if I was perfect, but one slip up and the effects were far worse than before. From what I could tell, I was getting more sick, not better. What I was doing was only masking the real problem, not healing it. I didn't know what the real problem was, but I wanted to figure it out.

I couldn't help but believe everything I was dealing with was related. But the more I learned online or in books, the more I found conflicting and confusing information. Every study seemed to be swayed one way or the other, depending on who ran the study, the marketer, and the product needing leverage. Each article seemed to have ulterior motives. I was entirely at a loss of what to do. I spent years at this point reading anything I could. Nothing held the answers for me that I was searching for. I felt like I had prayed an endless amount of prayers until one day, one very seemingly insignificant day, I finally received the answer I was looking for.

I was sitting at a new friend's house talking about our lives and getting to know each other. She smiled at me as I spoke, and before I left, she handed me a book.[37]

"Have you ever heard of him?" She asked.

"No," I said.

"Borrow this book, and let me know what you think." she said.

I had no idea what to expect. That night, I put my kiddos to bed early and began reading simply out of curiosity with zero expectations. The Author, Anthony William, began by telling a story about a voice speaking into his ear as early as 4 years old.

He was sitting at a dinner table with his family, and the voice told him to inform his grandmother that she had lung cancer. His grandmother was entirely symptom-free. She was startled enough to go and get checked anyway. Sure enough, she found out she did in-fact have cancer. He told his life story of having this spirit constantly by his side, teaching him of medical conditions and the healing foods placed on the plane to help our misinformed generation to heal.

It was everything I had been searching for. I couldn't stop reading. My heart was burning with love and gratitude, and I could tell it was the right book for me. I felt as if God himself had sat down with me on my couch and answered the questions I've had about my own body; what was wrong and how to heal it. Anthony William spoke of autoimmune conditions being a myth; that our bodies will never attack themselves; that they are fighting endlessly to try to help us and usually what they are up against is a virus.

I learned about the Epstein-Barr virus and its links to thyroid issues. I learned about my liver and how the virus affects the liver. I learned that sugar was the messenger that got blamed for the problem, but that adrenal fatigue and fat build-up in my liver was the real cause of my blood sugar issues. More importantly, I learned exactly what foods would feed and fight off the virus and what foods were created to heal it all.[38]

Everything I read made so much sense. My spirit had been whispering many of those exact things for years. I read all night long and finished the 344 pages the next afternoon. When I closed the last page, I held the book next to my heart, let tears fall freely down my face, and thanked God that such a book existed.

I immediately began to make changes. I got over my fear of fruit and higher-carb vegetables. I replaced my fridge full of meat, dairy, and low-carb foods with a fridge full of colorful fruits and veggies. It was as if in an instant, a fog was lifted off of my eyes. Looking at my now very colorful fridge, I was wildly aware of how mistaken I was—like someone had woken me up from a bad dream. I could visually see that these foods were healing foods. I started drinking celery juice in the mornings, having big fruit smoothies (which taste delicious, by the way), salads in the afternoon, and all the steamed vegetables I had been taught to fear or limit. I went from consistently restricting myself at every meal, to filling my body up with incredibly nourishing foods that left me feeling satisfied.

It wasn't long before I could tell that my body was healing. Only this time it was not slow, imperceptible, "healing". It was noticeable and rapid healing. In a relatively short amount of time, I lost large amounts of swelling. My nails began to grow thicker and stronger. My hair loss started growing back in. My acne cleared up. The thick callused skin (that I thought was hereditary) thinned out and started to have a healthy glow to it. My blood sugar levels were regulated, and each time I went to the doctor for check-ups my thyroid medication dose was lowered! (Hallelujah!) I was the witness to my own healing.

One of my favorite days was the day I sat in my doctor's office and finally heard those blessed words, "You could probably stop taking your medication if you wanted to."

I did what they said would never happen.

So why am I telling you all of this? Because I can imagine that some of you can relate. So many people are on medication and have been told their bodies cannot or will not heal. And you guys, I'm just not buying it! Bodies heal. When you get cut, your body immediately begins the healing process and continues until the skin is like new. Bones heal. Hell, even teeth heal! (Yes, I've reversed and completely healed my own cavities.) Our bodies get hurt, yes, and then they heal. I believed this while I was sick and I believe it even more now. Chronic illness, anxiety, clinical depression, and

PTSD symptoms can all heal. We only need to know what to do to aid our bodies in this healing process.

If you are struggling with your health, if you feel like you've searched the ends of the earth for answers, my plea to you is to not give up! If you have received answers to your questions and they don't feel like answers at all; if you feel deep within you that there has to be something more than what you have found, keep looking! I believe firmly that you feel that way for a reason. There *are* answers and healing *is* possible! Keep going until you've found what is right for *you*. Your journey to good health is worth every second of research, effort, and investment because it does impact your life deeply.

Make your physical health a priority.

I also want you to be aware of the fact that when we go through traumatic events, our body takes a terrible hit. Adrenaline surges through our veins, we lose sleep, we forget to eat, emotions are bottled up, hearts race, and the whole thing is a lot for a body to take—especially if the stress is long term. It is not uncommon for illness to pop up after traumatic events, so this is my reminder to you to take care of yourself! Be gentle—especially if you are going through something difficult. Give yourself permission to make your physical health a priority. Learn to listen to it. Learn to give it the right foods, proper amounts of rest, sunshine, fresh air, water, and attention.

Be willing to make changes.

Now I understand that not everyone has medical conditions they're worried about, so dramatic changes aren't always necessary. But I do want you to start noticing your own physical body. Connect with it and show up for it. Be willing to make changes, even if they are small changes. Do you notice you get a belly ache every time you drink beer and eat pizza? If so, start picking something else to put in your mouth! Do you notice you get a migraine every time you stay up too late? Set an alarm on your phone and go to bed earlier. Do you notice that every time you go for a run you feel less anxiety throughout the day? Start making the gym a part of your daily routine. Changes like this take a little grit at first, yes, but *there is no indulgence that feels better than a body in good health.*

If you are struggling with your physical body, these things are important to remember:

1. **Your health journey will look different from mine.**
   My one concern for sharing my story was that you might do what I did, no questions asked. I want to make it clear that I am not advising you to go against your doctor's advice. His or her advice might very well be perfect for you and exactly what you were looking for! If so, keep going with that. I only want to give you permission to follow your gut, and work with him/her to find your own path for healing. Trust yourself. There is so much that plays into physical health, including viruses, bacteria, heavy metals, chemicals, genetics, vitamins, minerals, herbs, nutrients, emotion, beliefs, etc. Your journey to healing your body will take you through learning about a number of these things. I only want to encourage you to keep going until you have found the level of healing you desire.

2. **God is willing to help, and will send you signs, symbols, and inklings. Trust Him.**
   I remember praying in the very beginning for guidance. Do you know what came up in prayer for me over and over and over? Fruit smoothies for breakfast, liver cleansing herbs such as dandelion, and eliminating harsh chemicals wherever possible. Go figure.

Whenever I was eating a bunch of high-fat foods, such as nuts or oils, I didn't feel great. I would have this thought in my mind of how rare and difficult it is to have that much oil in nature. A single nut is small, and each one is surrounded by a tough shell that takes exertion to open. Never in the history of time did they have large bags of ground-up nuts to make large loaves of bread or cakes out of. As I would pour entire cups of olive oil for these "healthy treats" I would think of how hard it would have been back in the day to have pressed enough olives for the amount of oil I was consuming in a day. I couldn't help but wonder if there was symbolic meaning in the way God had packaged certain foods and if they were meant to be eaten in the portions He provided.

Have you ever wondered about how foods look like what they are good for? A carrot, if cut in half, looks like an eye. As we know, they are a healing food for eyesight. A tomato looks like a heart and even has four chambers. Tomatoes are good for your heart. Pomegranate juice has a rich and deep pigment of scarlet. Pomegranates are a powerful blood cleanser and replenisher. Walnuts look like a brain and are even packaged in a hard cranium-like shell. We know these healthy oils in the right amounts are good for the brain. There are symbols everywhere in nature, trying to teach us how to heal. I feel that we are missing out immensely by looking past them for our answers.

If I could pass on a lesson, it would be this: trust yourself, your intuition, and your answers from God over what you might hear or read on the internet. He knows what He is doing. He created our bodies and the foods to go with them in the first place.

3. **There is no such thing as perfection.**

In all of my efforts to heal what ailed me, I failed to remember there is no such thing as arriving. We are living in a fallen world with mortal bodies. They are going to get sick once in a while, we are going to get hurt, and our bodies will grow older no matter how hard we try to slow the process. In all of your efforts, don't forget to allow yourself grace. We are all imperfect. I'm one dedicated girl and you bet your bottom dollar I still indulge in ice cream with my kiddos and a mean pizza night once in a while. I am not perfect, nor do I claim to be. What I am is improving. I am learning to love and care for my physical body one day at a time.

There will never be a day when you reach this perfect state of health and you don't have to worry about it ever again. Like a plant, your body will need constant nourishment from you until the day you die. This is a lifelong marathon, not a sprint. Developing habits that are sustainable is the best thing you can do. Start slow. Pick one thing and master it, then choose another. Get a buddy on board to hold you accountable and keep making baby steps. Allow yourself the time it takes to master each new habit.

If I could recommend another book I've loved it is called *Food Freedom Forever*, by Melissa Hartwig.[39] She is a girl entirely dedicated to her health, so much so that she developed the Whole30 program and has built a business and life around it. I can imagine you've heard of her. She also still enjoys her mother's baking around the holidays and a good cupcake once in a while WITHOUT BEATING HERSELF UP for it! She indulges with joy and then gets back on track to feeding her body the way she consciously intends to. We all could learn a thing or two from her thoughts on food freedom.

4. **Skinny doesn't equal healthy.**

In all of my efforts to overcome some of my illnesses, I've been confronted with the same reaction from others, "You don't need to be on a diet. You're already skinny." As if being skinny were all that mattered!

Being skinny did not mean I was healthy. Being skinny did not mean I had the energy to care for my growing babies. Being skinny did not mean that my organs, blood, and endocrine system were working correctly. *Being skinny does not mean you are in good health and risking your health in order to be skinny IS NOT WORTH IT.*

To any of you out there restricting the things your body desperately needs in order to be skinny, I would say that you cannot deprive yourself into wellness. Glowing health is achieved through love, nourishment, and giving your body what it needs to thrive. That includes indulging frequently in the most healing foods on the planet and getting plenty of rest, sunshine, water, and love.

5. **And finally, your body was not created to satisfy other's eyes. It was created to serve you.**

    Your body was created to care for you and carry you throughout your life. It was created to bless you with eyesight, touch, hearing, smell, and taste. It was created to carry your children; to hug, to laugh, to cry. It was created to squish your toes in warm sand; to tickle a giggling toddler; to witness the beauty of a sunset, and to smell fresh strawberries recently picked. Your body was not created to please others' eyeballs. It was God's gift to you, for you.

    Learn to tune out the opinions of others, whether they think you are too big or too small, too this or too that. No matter how hard you try, the size, shape, or color of your body will never satisfy the unsatisfiable. Ignore them and love your body as if it were your best friend. Listen when it asks you to slow down. Rest when you know you need rest. Be kind. Say nice things to yourself about yourself. Stick up for your body when other people don't recognize its worth. Let yourself have fun at swim parties or the lake, even when your imperfection shows in a swimsuit. Let your rounder parts wiggle as you dance. Let yourself squeal when you're excited and melt into your lover's arms at the end of a long day. I let my body be human because that is exactly what she is.

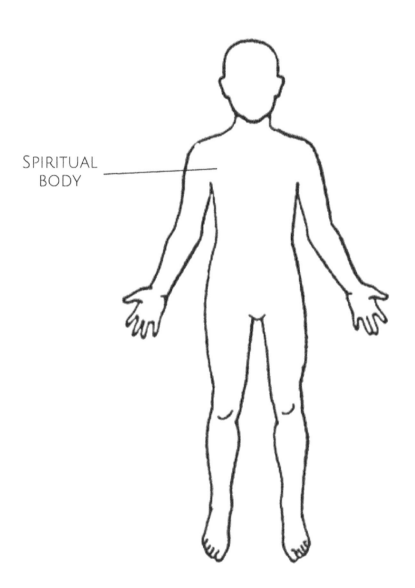

SPIRITUAL
BODY

9

SPIRITUAL BODY

As my physical health has improved, I've become more aware of the spirit that accompanies my physical body. You may have heard before, *we are spiritual beings, having an earthly experience.* We were first spirits; all of us. Every living thing—every human, animal, and plant existed as individual spirits before this earth was created. Our spirit is older, wiser, and therefore, a more powerful force to tap into if we are brave enough to spend time with it.

We forget about how important our spirits are until we watch as a spirit leaves a body. I hope not to trigger emotions with that last sentence, but I want you to tap into the visual of what a body is like without its spirit. You've seen that before. It is not the person. It is just the house. It was meant to age in this life and eventually die, while the spirit lives on.

Now I want you to put your hand on your chest. Feel your beating heart. Know that there is a physical heart beating and a spiritual heart. There are two. Our spiritual bodies are made similarly to our physical bodies. We would do ourselves a great service to learn about how to care for them.

Ironically, I learned about my spiritual body while in massage school. Do you remember the "S" shaped arm I got from snowboarding? Unfortunately, that accident happened while in massage school. I was a determined girl who had promised myself when school started that I'd never miss a class. So after surgery, I had my step-mom drive me home for class. I spent a few days giving one-armed massages with pins in my arm underneath my cast. I was in a lot of pain and could hardly move my fingers so as to not disturb the pins in my arm. There was a magic spot if I held my arm just right that would keep the pins away from the edge of my cast. I kept my arm there at all costs.

One day my teacher pulled me aside and asked if she could work on my arm. She must have sensed my fear of her hurting me because she comforted me by saying "I don't need to touch it." Intrigued, I offered her my arm. I spent the next 5 or so minutes in awe as she closed her eyes and ran her hands about an inch above the outside of my cast. She worked her way around in a circular motion pulling from the elbow down through the wrist and down through my fingers. In the end, she flicked my fingertips as if she was flicking away the pain out of my arm. Then she shook her hand out and began again.

She had this peaceful look on her face that calmed me, and my arm felt warm. For about an hour after she worked on me, I could feel buzzing throughout my arm. Even though everything she was doing was about an inch above my cast, I could feel what she was doing deep into the center of my bones underneath it. When she finished up, she asked how my arm was doing. I gave it a little wiggle and was amazed at how much more movement I had. I risk sounding dramatic here, but the truth is that the pain was almost entirely gone. I could move my arm back and forth against my cast, and it didn't hurt anymore! I was amazed!

She had taught me that day that our physical and spiritual bodies are so closely connected that sometimes it is hard to differentiate the two; that when one is injured, the other can be injured right along with it. While the doctor had done all he could to correct my physical injury, she was doing what she could to help with the trapped emotion—the spiritual injury. I had no idea up until that point that I could injure my spirit.

Later that year, we went into greater depth and practice with the idea of working on a person's spirit along with their physical body. We were taught about phantom pain, which occurs in 90-98% of amputees.[40] Did you know that when a person loses a limb, they'll usually still experience the physical sensation of having their limb, even after it's gone? What is even more incredible is that if they suffered from arthritis or some condition, they can still experience the pain of the ailment even without the physical limb. We were taught in school how to feel these things; how to sense the more refined and pure matter that exists where mortal matter once was.[41] We could feel buzzing, sometimes hot or cold pockets, and we would work to alleviate pain in these areas just as my teacher helped me alleviate my pain. I can't say that I'm good at giving it, but I've kept spiritual healers that practice different modalities nearby since that day. Just as I go to a regular massage therapist when I get kinks in my back and neck, I go to those who specialize in spiritual healing when my spirit is having a hard time releasing certain emotions or experiences.

I want to share one more story. Years later, I volunteered with some friends at an orphanage in Mexico. While we were there, I remember standing outside before we went in and being taught about the kids. They cautioned us to be careful about how we held them because many of them had suffered sexual abuse. They explained that to be held a certain way was triggering for them. I immediately connected that moment to my previous experience and knew that even though their physical wounds may have long since been healed, their spiritual wounds were still hurting.

I wondered how many people are walking around with trapped emotions creating raw wounds in their spirits with no idea that they are there because they cannot see them.

Most likely, all of us do. I wished at that moment that we all had the eyes to see each other's spirits. I think we would have a lot more compassion, gentleness, and patience with each other.

There is one other aspect of our spirits, beyond the fact that they exist and can be injured, that is important to discuss. The spiritual body communicates with the physical body. This specific interaction is called conscience. Just as we all have spiritual bodies, we all have this communication that tells us right and wrong. It's innate. It's reliable and steady, and we are born with it. This is not just an echo of what our parents told us is right and wrong. It is much deeper and much more personal than that. Outside opinions can't change it. You know things on a level that isn't alterable.

As I've written this book and reflected on my story, I've thought to myself, "Why were my younger years so painful? My story is not unique. A lot of kids go through a divorce. A lot of people drink, especially during their younger years. So what was the big deal? Why was it such an awful experience?" Here is what I know: I was living outside of my conscience. I knew what I was doing was not for me.

Living outside of our conscience is living in our own personal hell. We can't escape it. No one can convince us otherwise. The whole world could tell you that something is okay, but if you know it's not right for you and you do it anyway, you will feel pain. To contrast that, I'll add that to live according to your own conscience, or your spirit's truth, is to live in peace. Everyone could hate you for a decision, but if you know it is right for you, there is a sense of stillness in knowing everything will be okay.

Be aware of negative spirits.

This is one of those things that might seem creepy, but it is a reality. There are a lot of people who have lived and died on this earth and there are a lot of spirits who never came. They are all around us. Some are good spirits and some are darker.

If you have ever tried to make a big change in your life for the better, you may have felt them. These evil spirits are hell-bent on keeping you stuck, sad, and lonely. They distract us from the good we intend to do. They keep us from reaching out. They whisper garbage in our ears that isn't true. You may have felt at times that you are stuck, overwhelmed with negativity, or have a dark cloud over you. This very well could be these negative spirits that are sent to distract, discourage, and deceive you.[42] They are real. Whether you can see them or not, you need to know they are not a figment of your imagination.

The most annoying thing about them is that *they whisper things in your own voice* and make you think it is you. The scriptures say, *"Others he flattereth away and telleth them there is no hell; and he saith unto them: I am no devil, for there is none- and thus he whisperer in their ears until he grasps them with his awful chains."*[43]

He denies his existence and speaks in first person, saying in your own voice, "*I am....*" and then speaks lies; "*I am dumb. I am unworthy. I am not loved. I am an awful person.*" THIS IS NOT YOU! It's him. It's them. You are God's child. You are loved. You are special. Please recognize these voices as they come and know they are not yours.

There are spirits all around us, and they wait for any open invitation they can get. They wait until we are weak, or lonely, or afraid, and they hop on into our space, filling us with despair.

The good news is that you have the body, and it is yours, so you have the power to tell them to leave. I can't stress how important it is to tell them to leave and to tell them often. While you might feel like an idiot speaking to some unseen world, it is worth it if you are free from their pull on you. Once you figure them out, they are afraid and weakened. Tell them to go out loud and in a firm voice. Feel free to call upon your faith in the Lord to say something such as, "In the name of Jesus Christ, I command you to leave." then notice how the darkness surrounding you lifts. These spirits know they must go.

Every time I do this, I try to fill the space back up with light and peace. I'll turn on good music, I'll repeat affirmations in my mind, I'll say a prayer. You get the idea...

When these negative voices come, and they will when you are feeling weak, remind yourself that you are a son or daughter of God. You have infinite potential. You are perfectly loved by someone with an infinite amount of grace. You are smart. You are worthy. You are loved. You are a good person. We resist the devil with the truth. These statements are the truth. You are a living being that is allowed imperfection to grow. Trust that you are loved. Know that you are loved. Speak up to these negative thoughts that say otherwise.

"Resist the devil and He shall flee from you."

-James 4:7[44]

Throughout the rest of this book, you will do a lot of listening to your own heart and spirit. But before you do, you need to know that it's actually *your* spirit you're listening to. Discouragement, despair, darkness, these are not you. Tell the negative spirits to leave first, and you will find better answers.

Once you have created this safe space, feel free to invite your guardian angels to be with you as you learn to heal your spiritual body. Again, your healing will be specific to you, but to share some wisdom I've gained along the way, Here are some healing practices to adopt:

1. **Go frequently to the source that created your spirit.**
   Someone created you. Getting to know that some-one is like getting to know yourself in a whole new light. Getting to know God is a very natural healing process; like a soothing medicinal balm to an aching soul. Like a dying plant that is finally placed in the sun, you will feel things with Him that feel a lot like coming home.

2. **Be still.**
   Your spirit doesn't shout. It will not compete for attention. It waits quietly until you are alone. Take time to listen to that inner voice. Pay attention. Let what your spirit says matter more to you than other people's opinions. The more you listen, appreciate, and heed its advice, the easier it gets to discern it.

3. **Spend time alone in quiet meditation.**
   I do a specific meditation to help me find blocks or injuries to my spirit. I usually do this one sitting up or standing. I close my eyes, breathe deeply for a minute, and then I imagine light pouring in through the top of my head, through my brain, my ears, my eyes, down my neck, and into my body. I feel as the light flows through every part of me and notice how well it is flowing.

   There are parts of me that the light moves through effortlessly. My mind and my heart almost always soak it up like a sponge. Then there are other areas where I feel the light slow down or get stuck. My hips, knees, and feet are a common place that is either blocked or takes time to let the light through. I've had blocks there for years, and it's something I'm still learning about and working on.

   I try to send love to those parts of my body, be aware of them, and get help with them. It's a process that requires patience, but I love that meditation and the way it makes me feel.

4. **Create.**

Again, pain in the spiritual body is often caused by trapped emotions. So releasing trapped emotions is healing to your spirit. Creating art is a powerful way to release trapped emotions. I teach and practice therapeutic art for this very purpose. The rules: No judging yourself and do whatever comes to you without thinking. Just like you did when you were a kid. If you'd like a surefire way to hear your own spirit talk to you, sit down, shut your mind off, and start to color. As you get into the flow of it, start noticing, *what is my spirit doing here? What are the colors saying, what are the movements I'm making? What is this emotion?* As you start asking questions, thoughts will come into your mind and your spirit will explain things to you that you didn't know you knew. Write what you hear, do what it says. I can't explain how or why this works but it does. Somehow creating this way opens the doors for communication between my mind and soul effortlessly. (For more info on this check out my website for Therapeutic Art classes or my TEDxIdahoFalls talk titled: How I Found Healing Through Honest Creativity.[45])

5. **Do things that strengthen your spirit.**

Remember, our spirits are older and wiser than our bodies are. They've been around a lot longer. Our spirits will long for things that our body doesn't want to do. For instance, your spiritual body will long for a healthy lifestyle while your physical body might want to sit on the couch and binge-watch Netflix and eat brownies! Every time you choose to forego the brownies and go for a run, your spirit becomes stronger.

6. **Allow your feelings as they come.**

I know I've talked about this plenty already, but the health of your spirit needs to let your feelings flow through without getting stuck. An emotion is just a vibra-tion. *Your spirit can handle vibrations.* What it doesn't like is for these vibrations to stick around in one spot for years. Let them flow through you instead.

7. **And finally, stay away from things that make you feel like crap.**

I try not to watch shows or look at or read things that make my spirit feel dark. I seek out things that bring peace into my life, and I purposely search for the light. This takes a concerted effort because we are constantly bombarded by negativity, but it can be done. To heal our spirits, we need to find and bask in the warmth of the light.

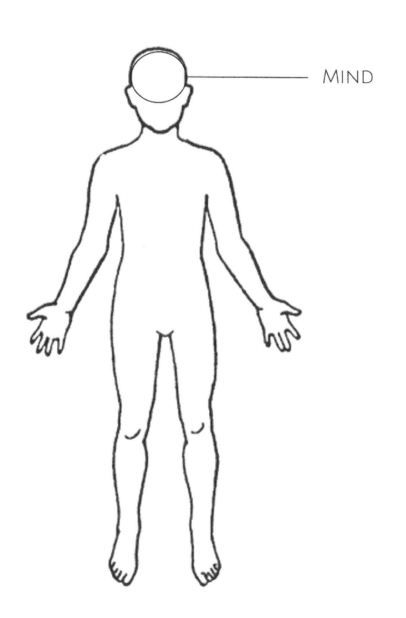

MIND

10

MIND

Our minds are the most powerful and sometimes the most detrimental power in our lives. Learning to understand yours, specifically, can move very large mountains in your healing process. Everything begins in the mind with a thought. Anything ever created was first created with thought. You, personally, can create very special and important things for yourself and others if you will first be brave enough to take your mind there.

Our mental health is so important I could have easily begun here, but I needed you to understand the physical and spiritual for you to understand that you can train your mind to be tuned to either one. Like tapping into the proper wavelength or radio station, your mind can be tuned to either spending more time in what it has already experienced (physical) or creating something new (spiritual).

To have an untrained mind, or a mind only aware of the physical, is to experience everything on a lesser level. Remember—physical matter is younger. Your physical body or physical mind is only as old as you are. Our physical minds are like rambunctious teenagers, when left unsupervised or "unconscious" they run wild. They come up with all sorts of crazy stories and explanations for things and we are left believing whatever they say, no matter how untrue the thought may be.

On the other hand, our spiritual minds, or a mind more tuned to spiritual matter, is much more mature. It understands things we may not fully comprehend with our physical mind. It is often more quiet, peaceful, and brave. It requires you to be more quiet, peaceful, and brave to communicate well with you.

When we hear something true, this part of our mind says *"Yes! I knew that already!"* The spiritual mind has knowledge that is organized, pure, and unending. It knows without a doubt that you have value. It knows your potential. It knows who you are and what you were meant to come to earth to do. The physical mind can be swayed. Like opposite ends of a pendulum swing, the physical mind can be all over the place. The spiritual mind, however, stays locked in its place. It is steady in the truth.

Our physical mind runs especially wild when we feel threatened, rejected, or go through something traumatic. Therefore, we need to do the most work surrounding these experiences. Our brains like to take one experience and turn it into a blanket statement. For instance, if you were treated poorly by someone of the opposite sex, it's quick to believe that all men or women are that way. It takes work to quiet the mind and tap into the truth, but it is absolutely worth every ounce of effort.

Getting right with your mental health should be high on your priority list if you want to transform your life into something that is healthy and happy. In his book, *Stillness is the Key*, Ryan Holiday says, *"That space between your ears—that's yours. You don't just have to control what gets in, you also have to control what goes on in there. You have to protect it from yourself, from your own thoughts. Not with sheer force, but rather with a kind of gentle, persistent sweeping. Be the librarian who says "Shhh!" to the rowdy kids, or tells the jerk on his phone to please take it outside. Because the mind is an important and sacred place. Keep it clean and clear."*[46]

Getting to know your own mind takes work. Becoming aware of your thoughts and dismissing the unproductive ones can be a full-time job. Learning habitual thoughts and forming new ones takes concentrated effort and mental sweat.

I imagine our thought patterns are like paths in the woods. A well-worn path is easy to follow, and we tend to stick with it, whether it is the correct way or not. When we wake up and realize these thoughts are leading us to feel and do miserable things, we have to step off the trail and start forming another. Think of how hard it is to make new paths in the woods. You'll need tools to get through some of the debris. It'll take time and effort, but with consistency, you can create better thought-patterns that are more in line with your goals.

✿

Remember the stories we talked about earlier? Becoming aware of your stories is the goal here. If mental health is what you desire, it is important to examine the stories you are telling yourself regularly.

Other healing practices to adopt:

1. **Gratitude**

    I know of no other practice that will transform your mind and life more quickly than that of finding gratitude. Rhonda Byrne says, "When you're grateful for the things you have, no matter how small they may be, you will see those things instantly increase."[47] We get more of what we are grateful for. Gratitude unlocks joy and happiness. It is the key to release us from the prison of our depressed and downtrodden minds. Count your blessings as often as possible. Keep the things you love front and center; embrace them, magnify them, and watch as miracles begin to happen.

2. **Mental inventories**

Out of curiosity, sometimes I'll pick a random topic and sit down and write what I believe about the said topic. I have a notebook with a topic written at the top of each page (i.e. money, men, women, my mom, etc.). I'll pick a topic that has been on my mind and write every thought that comes up in my head about it, no matter how absurd. Sometimes I am shocked to see my thoughts on paper! Sometimes I laugh out loud. Sometimes I'm embarrassed. Always, I learn something new. Afterward, I'll sit over the paper entirely filled with random thoughts and cross off every sentence that isn't true or not worth my time believing anymore. I'm amazed at how little is left sometimes! Then, I flip the paper over and rewrite what I *want* to believe, and what is actually true. (Hint: If a thought makes you miserable, it's probably not entirely true.) I'll then go back and read the true statements throughout the day and week. Sometimes I'll put them on my wall for a while to engrain them more deeply in my mind.

3. **Life-long learning**

I read books and listen to a lot of podcasts on mental health. My favorite at the moment is Brooke Castillo's *The Life Coach School* podcast.[48] She is brilliant at helping a person realize that they really do get to choose what they think. She repeatedly explains that we get to make circumstances mean whatever we want them to mean by what we think about them. She is a master of her mind and has such a simple and happy way of teaching others how to master theirs too. I love this idea that we should be telling our brains what to think, instead of the other way around.

4. **Hypnotherapy**

In all my years of seeking out mental health, I will tell you the most powerful, quick, and long-lasting therapy I have ever received has been from hypnotherapy. Some things are so deeply rooted in our subconscious that there is only so much we can do from talking about it. Hypnotherapy reaches those memories that are so deep you do not consciously remember them. When you are made aware of these thoughts, you can address and clear them up. What has taken me years to figure out in other avenues took me one or two sessions in hypnotherapy for it to clear up and stay clear.[49]

5. **Slow down.**

I've tried to live life slow enough that I can breathe deeply and hear myself think throughout the day. I check in with myself, especially when I feel anxiety or fear. I'll ask myself, *"Hey Heather, how come you're stressed? What're you thinking about?"* And then I listen. Sometimes I'll recognize that I just imagined something terrible happening that isn't actually happening! I acknowledge to myself that it was a trail of thought based on fear, and I reassure myself of something more positive. While this process sounds exhausting, I promise it gets easier as you grow more familiar with your own mind.

6. **Get back in the driver's seat.**

I put my mind to work throughout the day. I give it a task and put it to work to create what I want. Almost every morning, I wake up and look at images of what I want and then use my mind to imagine it coming true. Almost every night, I try to imagine the following morning and mentally create the next day. A mind without a task is like a teenager without parents! Be the parent.

Remember that every single part of you is living. It is not set in stone to remain as it is. If you recognize that your mind is weak, you can strengthen it. Just as a dirty house can be cleaned after a party, so can your mind be picked up and polished. It's not a one-time event. It's a lifelong practice of picking up as life goes about getting it dirty. It's setting your bar a little bit higher for yourself and deciding you want to start thinking thoughts that set you free.

7. **Avoid jumping to conclusions.**

Our minds really, really love answers. They want to know what everything means, and they want to know now! The reality of life is, though, that when things happen, we don't always know why. We need to allow ourselves the space of not knowing.

There is a Chinese Proverb that goes something like this: "A farmer and his son had a beloved stallion who helped the family earn a living. One day, the horse ran away, and their neighbors exclaimed, "Your horse ran away, what terrible luck!" The farmer replied, "Maybe so, maybe not. We'll see."

A few days later, the horse returned home, leading a few wild mares back to the farm as well. The neighbors shouted out, "Your horse has returned, and brought several horses home with him. What great luck!" The farmer replied, "Maybe so, maybe not. We'll see."

Later that week, the farmer's son was trying to break one of the mares, and she threw him to the ground, breaking his leg. The villagers cried, "Your son broke his leg, what terrible luck!" The farmer replied, "Maybe so, maybe not. We'll see."

A few weeks later, soldiers from the national army marched through town, recruiting all the able-bodied boys for the army. They did not take the farmer's son, still recovering from his injury. Friends shouted, "Your boy is spared, what tremendous luck!" To which the farmer replied, "Maybe so, maybe not. We'll see."[50]

The farmer was wise to wait, to not get worked up about every event. He knew there was always more to the story and his story wasn't over yet. We would be wise to follow his example in learning to give space for life to unfold.

I've mentioned before that the facts are neutral, and it is our mind that carries on with the story. I'd like to push the envelope even further with the idea that with Christ, all facts will be in the *positive* one day. ALL things we go through in this life will be for our experience and for our ultimate good.

If you have a mind like mine that wants to come to a conclusion about all the things right now, decide ahead of time that ALL things are working out for your good; ALL things are great "luck".

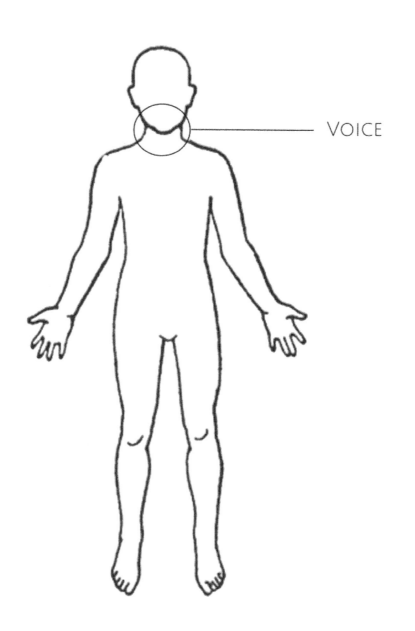

VOICE

11

VOICE

Our voice is something many of us quiet for fear of what others might think. We keep our unique personalities bottled up because we aren't sure we'll fit in. In more primitive days, being different could mean you would be kicked out of the group, left to fend for yourself in the wild. Because of this ancient fear of survival, our brains have taught us to fear what is different about us. What's a shame about that is that *whatever makes you different is the gift you are meant to share with the world.*

Our generation is living in a stage of higher consciousness where these old ideas are falling away. The shame you have felt in your past about the things that make you different are no longer serving you. People are longing for your gifts, unique perspectives, and honest story. Being brave enough to share your voice takes vulnerability. As someone being vulnerable right now at this very moment, I will tell you it is worth it!

There was a time in my life where I was silent; I mean, I talked to people all the time, but I never really said anything that mattered. I hid everything about me that was unique. Being a good Christian girl was who I wanted to be, so I surrounded myself with people who strengthened me in that. But there was also so much more to who I was, and because those things felt different, I hid them. I judged every part of me through someone else's eyes and became this watered-down version of myself, afraid to speak. What I'm realizing now is that my past has given me a unique perspective that might be worth sharing.

I know now that I see things differently. I don't see "sin" as a great fault or offense. I see it as distance. I don't see me or you, I see us—a family. I don't see superiority in the color of skin, size, or shape of a body—I see beauty in being alive. I don't see my religion as the only way to live this life, I see the importance of coming to know God through our own experiences. I believe in agency and the freedom to learn through making mistakes. I believe in the freedom to be. Be different. Be inquisitive. Be brave. Be willing to not know. We are all unique. We are all on the discovery of finding out who we are and what we are here to do.

We were sent here on this earth for a reason—to experience pleasure and pain, health and sickness, joy, and sorrow; all of which will serve us; all of which is necessary for a fulfilling life. We are meant to think differently, to act differently, to have different hair, and like different food. We are meant to talk differently, laugh differently, and have our own personality.

Having this courage to be different is something I'm still working on every day. Recovering from people-pleasing has been harder for me than any other addiction. If I'm being honest, I'm still breaking through my walls, getting to know myself, and speaking my truth.

One of the reasons this book has taken me so long to write is because of that one thing—my voice. What do I want to spend time saying? And do I dare say it? This book has been a brave step in me sharing my unique voice. *It is unique,* I know that. And it is evolving. I'm still discovering myself. I'm still discovering what it is I want to share with the world.

Out of curiosity, I looked up the average life expectancy today. On wickipedia.com, the average life expectancy in 2020 for the United States is 78.9 years.[51] That gives me roughly 46 years left, according to this study. Forty-six years! That's if everything goes well, and God permits.

I have already spent 32 years of my life showing up mostly in survival mode. I don't want to waste the rest. I want to spend my remaining years raising my voice for something good and doing good for others. I don't know everything about why I'm here and what I'm meant to do, but I know for sure of one gift I've found and want to share. If I had to condense it down to one word, that word would be 'healing'.

If I could shout one thing from the rooftops, it would be that healing is possible. Healing is probable. Healing is available. Healing is within reach. I want to take every person I know by the hand, look in their eyes, and tell them not to give up; that life gets better as we gain the knowledge we need to overcome our hard times.

So what about you? Approximately how many years do you have left? If you could spend those years raising your voice to say anything, what would it be?

One word

I love condensing things down into one word. I want you to think for a minute about your social media accounts if you have them. If you could condense what you're saying on social media into one word, what would it be? Is that what you want to say? Are you speaking your truth? What about at home with your family? Do you raise your voice to argue, to find fault, or to lift? What about your job? One word—what would it be? What about your passion? In one word, what is it?

What is your passion?

If you could help anyone find one thing in this life, what would it be? Do not be surprised if what you feel passionate about was born out of your adversity. This very well could be your gift you were sent to give the world; a gift achieved by walking through the coals yourself.

Speaking up might very well take all you've got, but as you speak up, you will grow. The further you get along the healing journey, the stronger this voice will get.

I recently listened to an episode on the Medical Medium's Podcast titled, *Soul's Gold*.[52] In it, he talked about suffering, wounds, pain, losses, sorrow, hardships, trials, etc. being not what any of us choose, but when they visit us, we get our *greatest treasures*. Our hardships make us special, and with that specialness, we can change the world.

A voice beyond words

When I talk about your voice, it is important to explain that using your voice doesn't always mean speaking. While it can be an important part, there is something even more powerful—what you do.

What you do has more power than what you say. If you think you are not saying anything, think again. To be alive is to have a voice. Even if you are hiding in your room saying nothing, that speaks something about you. Your voice will always be more than words.

Ralph Waldo Emerson says, "What you do speaks so loudly that I cannot hear what you say."[53] Sometimes the most powerful things you will ever say will be said without words. Sometimes holding your ground, being still, standing up, sitting down, smiling, walking out of a room, or into a new one speaks plenty.

Your voice includes how you are showing up for yourself, your friends, your family, and for God. Do you like what you're saying? If not, what would you change?

The healing practices for this section might surprise you.

1. **Before you speak, be still.**

   In Proverbs 29:11 it says, "A fool uttereth all his mind, but a wise man keepeth it in till afterwards."[54] To have a healthy "voice" does not mean you say whatever you want, whenever you want. Because we have opinions, doesn't mean it's helpful to share them all the time or to try to convince other people to have the same ones.

   I think a very important part of raising your voice is to spend some time in silence, making sure what you are saying is actually what you want to use your energy saying. A healthy voice is selecting consciously how we want to show up in this world, and then bravely doing so, no matter how it's received.

   So before you speak, be quiet. Be alone. Drown out the voices around you to get to know your own. A voice used with power and dignity will be a voice in calm control.

   A journal is a helpful tool. Take time to decide what your core values are. What matters to you? As you discover these things, they will be a guide to you throughout your life.

2. **Start by changing your actions first.**

   To set me up for success, before shouting to the universe that I'm changing something, before announcing this to my friends, my family, and their dogs, I've learned instead to give myself a minute to develop the new habit first. Believe me, any new habit, no matter how simple, will take a hot minute to master. It'll take planning and discipline, so allow yourself grace as you grow into it.

My husband is really good at this. He sets goals that I never hear about, slays them, and lets his actions speak of it themselves. The guy rarely says a word about his accomplishments. Sometimes I wonder if staying quiet is almost a game he plays, like "*Let's see how long it takes her to notice.*" He is a prime example of moving forward until you're showing up differently.

3. **Decide whose opinion matters to you.**

It won't take long, or much growth on your end before you start to realize that the people around you are afraid of you changing. Why? I don't know, besides the fact that it shifts the way they measure and see themselves. Change is scary for everyone, and your changes will ruffle some feathers. It will. It doesn't matter what changes you make—your food, your hair, your job, where you live, your faith. Be prepared for someone to have an opinion about it.

In order for you to navigate this, there will come a point where you will be backed up against a wall and have to decide whose opinion matters to you and why. I'm telling you, the braver you are and the farther you spread your voice, the more comfortable you are going to have to be with people not liking you. No amount of perfection in the world could please these people. So you are going to have to get very specific about whose opinion matters to you and why. Let me just tell you that my list is having to get rather short these days.

4. **Get out there, and start being yourself.**

Don't make the mistake of living your whole life on this earth without anyone getting to know the real you.

To live all-in is to let yourself be seen and show up as your glorious self. You're allowed to have fun. You're allowed to play and try new things.

Think of a new baby that is discovering their hands for the first time. Think of how excited they are when they look in a mirror and get to know their own face. Allow yourself permission to admire yourself as a baby does. Take your time. Enjoy the discovery of the things that light you up. Notice what makes your little heart skip a beat. Notice what you are drawn to. Notice what makes you feel beautiful or alive and start there. Let yourself embrace your unique qualities.

Here's a personal example that is fairly weird—I'm obsessed with dreadlocks! A little part of my heart gets eeeeextra giddy about them. Do I know why? No! Even I'm confused about that, but I DO love them. I've spent hours upon hours and many failed attempts to find the right ones for me, but I can't deny that I love them. Haha. Have I said that already?

So what about you? What do you love? What is unique about you? What do you like that might be weird to someone else? Have you embraced it yet? Do you share who you are with the people around you, even when you know you're not perfect? Do you wear what makes you feel good, even if it's not what your friends wear? Do you eat what you like to eat, even if no one else agrees?

A friend was talking to me on the phone the other day and reminded me of something I desperately needed to hear. She said, "You don't need an explanation for why you love something or want to do something. "because I like it" or "because I want to" is a good enough reason." As you go out into this great big world, you might notice you don't fit someone else's mold, and that is the beauty of you. You don't have to.

Start showing up as the unique creature God intended you to be. Little by little, this will get easier. Little by little, you'll find yourself. Little by little, your unique voice will grow. And with your voice, you can change the world.

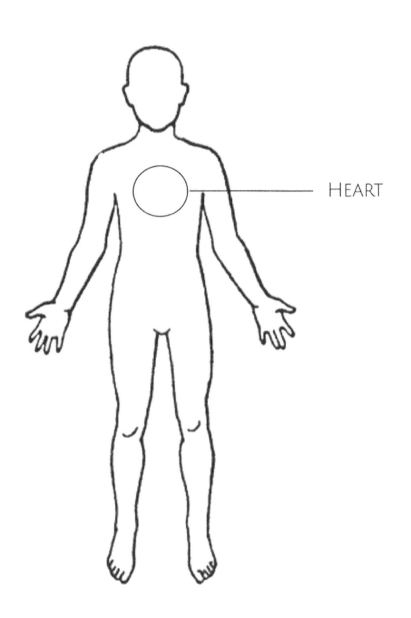

HEART

12

HEART

I n one click of a button, I just erased about five paragraphs on facts about the human heart. The physical heart is absolutely amazing! Volumes are written on the miracle of the human heart, but that is not what I feel I should focus on here.

There is, however, one study I want to talk about. It is the subject of *heart intelligence*. Scientists have discovered neurons in the heart similar to that of the brain. They have deemed the heart as "the little brain" and proven that it has the ability to think, learn, remember, and even sense our inner and outer worlds completely independent of the brain.[55]

Scientists are now recognizing that the knowledge from this "little brain" is more accurate. If we can learn to tap into communication with it, (which I will be teaching you to do), we will be led from a more pure and honest source. The heart is deeply intuitive, and these scientific findings prove the words of Robert Vallett that say, "*The human heart feels things the eyes cannot see, and knows what the mind cannot understand.*"[56]

Our hearts are the delicate, yet most central and power- ful part of us. They are where the physical and the spiritual meet. The physical heart beating is the first and last indicator of life. No matter how bleak your conditions may be, if your heart is beating inside of your chest, there is still hope, love, and life. No matter what has gone wrong, what you or anyone else has done, if your heart is beating, you are free to heal.

Your heart has to be the most courageous of all organs. As Rupi Kaur put it, "*What is stronger than the human heart which shatters over and over and still lives?*"[57] Our hearts, time and time again, bravely take on the contrast of the most devastating and the most breathtakingly beautiful moments in our lives; processing, storing, and communicating as it heals. Our hearts can handle things we never imagined were possible.

I want you to spend a moment and think of your own heart. What has it gone through for you? Who has it loved? Who has it lost? Who have you let in, and it hasn't gone the way you expected? Who do you wish you would have been brave enough to let in? What does it hope for? What does it believe? How long has it been beating for you?

Your physical heart truly is a best friend you didn't realize you had. It beat approximately 50 million times for you before you ever even took your first breath.[58]

It will continue to beat approximately 2 billion more times for you throughout your life, pushing healing blood full of oxygen and nutrients to nourish you with every pump.[59]

Your heart is a constant and unfailing friend; never resting, never giving up on you.

If I could have you sit in front of me, I would have you close your eyes, breathe, and imagine this heart beating in your chest for you. Feel free to place your hand where your heart is and feel its rhythm. Every beat is a symbol of love; that love is real; that love is continuing on. Despite all you have been through, love has never abandoned you. It was there whether you were aware of it or not, selflessly caring for you. Love is inside of you. It has always been there.

It takes a brave person to sit alone and be with his or her own heart; to feel and embrace whatever he/she may find there. Remember, your heart has intelligence and is a powerful force for good. Your mind will race with all sorts of crazy ideas, but your heart? Its answers are a little more pure. It will guide you throughout your life if you let it.

There will be moments where you feel that part of your spirit burn or have a swelling motion within your chest. Pay close attention to these feelings and what they are asking you to do. The mind and heart were created to work in harmony. If something is burning in your chest and your mind can confirm that it is good, I believe you should continue moving forward with confidence that you are on the right track, even if it doesn't make perfect sense.

There also may be times in your life where you feel that your heart is shut down and afraid to feel. When our hearts have been through a great deal, many of us will build walls around them. We will choose to not go to the depths of love or pain. We will choose to not let anyone in for a time. There can be a purpose to this. Some distance can act as protection as you strengthen and heal your wounds. As you become stronger, you'll become more confident. If you keep doing your work, you will be able to open the doors and windows to more people and experiences again.

When something is special and sacred, you protect it like a rose bush with thorns guarding its precious fruit. It's okay to learn who is safe with certain parts of your heart and only let certain people there. A sign of maturity is being wise enough to know who isn't safe inside the sacred chambers of your heart and to not open the doors no matter how loud they may knock. You are okay to do that. That does not make you mean—it makes you brave. Another sign of strength is being wise enough to let the good ones in, no matter how terrifying it may be to feel the magic of love again.

I will touch on feelings again for a moment. Feelings are powerful tools to show us where we are at. There are two types of feelings to be aware of: ones that flow freely like waves and others that are similar to an undercurrent. Some come and go as they please, often changing dramatically throughout the day. Others will linger under the surface for long periods of time.

Spend time getting familiar with these two types of feelings. Ask yourself throughout the day what your feelings are. There really is no right or wrong feeling. The goal isn't to change them; instead, it is about getting to know them. Part of healing your heart is allowing it to be where it is at and having compassion for whatever you find there. It's like getting to know a new friend you can't help but love already.

So how do you communicate with this heart? A lot of us have shut our hearts down. Our hearts are the feeling center of our lives, and a lot of us are afraid to feel. Take your time with this. Get to know the way your heart communicates with you. It is different from your mind. You won't hear words the same as your mind can hear words. Instead, you will *feel* them.

A heart's communication is a little more abstract. It loves colors and imagery and sounds. Your heart often responds with images when you talk to it. It loves dreams, art, and meditation for this reason. The next time you have a vivid dream that you feel has some significance, try asking your heart what it means. Get out a piece of paper and pen, connect with a higher power or your higher self it to be with you and teach you. Start writing things down that you saw in your dream and try to keep up as the interpretation flows into your consciousness. I can barely write fast enough when

I have done this! It is obvious to me in these moments that my heart has been dying to talk to me!

I guess I'm getting into healing practices already, so here we go…

Healing practices to adopt:

1. **Notice expansions and contractions.**

   A heart says "Yes" to something through opening up wide. You will feel warmth and a reaching out or an expansion feeling in your chest. A heart says "No" through contractions; through retracting inward, pulling back, closing up, and cooling down.

   Listen to these signs and honor your own heart by trusting it. In situations such as abuse, we have ignored these tender feelings to survive. The time is now yours to stand up for your own heart. Say "No" when it says "No". Be confident in these no's. Trust that your heart is a loyal friend. Let it speak to you. Let it be the companion you've been searching for.

2. **Practice yoga, particularly heart openers.**

   If you know there is a block in your heart, and you feel shut down or if you feel bitterness, anger, and jealousy frequently, try yoga. I've found yoga helpful, especially anything that stretches out my chest. Another great practice is to try doing yoga without any instructors or videos. Instead, use your heart as your guide. Just sit quietly on your mat, breathe, connect with your heart, and move slowly through stretches and poses that come to you. It doesn't need to be perfect, only let it come from within you, instead of someone else. Set a timer and try to stay on your mat the entire time.

3. **Meditate.**

   I love to lie on my back, spread my arms open wide, and imagine light pouring directly into my heart. I fill my entire body up, create a bubble around me, and then allow it to pour over—filling up my room, our home, the neighborhood we live in, the state we live in, the country, etc. until the whole world/universe is filled with love. Sometimes after that, I'll pick one person to focus on giving extra love to. I really like starting or ending the day with this meditation.

Another meditation I love is taking a mental walk. As I walk, I begin discovering things that my heart wants me to see. So this is how this one goes for me—I find a comfortable spot to lie down, relax my mind, take deep breaths, imagine each part of my body relaxing one by one (either head to toes or toes to head), and breathe again. I invite light, count down (5,4,3,2,1), getting deeper into relaxation with each number until at one, I completely surrender.

I then imagine myself walking into a garden or a forest. I keep walking and invite my heart to show me objects as I walk. I usually find around three things on this walk. One by one, I'll ask my heart about their meaning. I let the meditation guide me, not knowing beforehand what I'll find. Sometimes the objects make immediate sense, and sometimes I have to ask questions. I make sure to keep a notebook with me to write everything down and follow up with whatever my heart is asking me to do.

4. **Practice asking your heart questions instead of your mind.**

Sit somewhere quiet. (You might like to have a notebook nearby.)

Breathe and focus on your breath until your mind begins to quiet or slow down. Sometimes I'll move my head from side to side and imagine my thoughts falling to the earth.

Connect to your heart by focusing on it.

Think of grateful or loving thoughts until you feel a tingling or swelling sensation in your heart. This part is important. Focusing on gratitude and good thoughts get us in harmony with *truth* and *love*. It is like tuning your heart into the proper channel or wavelength for honest answers.

Ask it a question.

Notice expansions, contractions, and new thoughts accompanied by clear emotion.

You may be surprised by how quickly you receive answers that you may have been struggling with for years. I recently asked my heart a question that my brain has been questioning for so long. In writing this chapter, it dawned on me finally to ask a better source. The answer was so clear and simple that I laughed out loud.

5. **Incorporate journaling.**

Again, art journaling is a dream! I obviously love it because I keep talking about it! But if this seems too abstract, try putting your feelings into written words. Explaining your own feelings to yourself is an incredibly powerful healing tool. Get a lined notebook, or an online notebook, and practice telling the truth about how you feel. As you practice writing your true feelings rather than what you're 'supposed' to feel, you will get better and better at dealing with your emotions and explaining them to those around you.

6. **Focus on opening your heart up to those you love.**

Sometimes we know our heart is closing off due to past hurt or pain and not due to the person sitting in front of us at the present moment. This is when you have to choose vulnerability and love, despite the fear you may feel. Determine who it is in your life that you want to connect with and make a concerted effort to be connected with them. Tell them things you love about them that you wouldn't normally say. Tell them how you're feeling, even if you stumble in the process. These raw, real conversations will deepen your heart's ability to love.

7. **Practice choosing the most enjoyable emotions.**
While I do believe that we are meant to learn from all emotions, we can practice choosing the ones that feel nice. If you love the way it feels to be engulfed in love, try walking around today and point out everything you love. Focus on those things and watch them magnify in your life. Tell everyone you love that you love them and what it is you love about them. Spend time submerging yourself in these feelings. Notice as your heart expands, and your life improves.

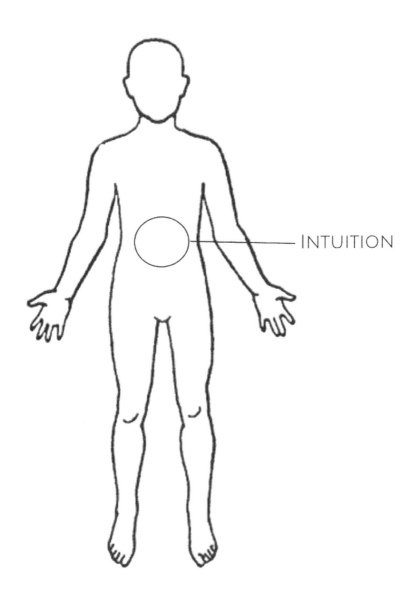

INTUITION

13

INTUITION

One time I went to a dance party. It was a non-alcoholic event, and my sister was driving, so naturally, I downed a bunch of alcohol before we met up and played it cool like I wasn't buzzing. When we got there, I made my way through the crowd in search of someone to keep me less lonely for the night. I spot him. He was wearing a red shirt and making his way out of the crowd. I grabbed his hand as if I needed it to make my way out too. We immediately connected and ended up hanging out all night together. I liked him, and I could tell he liked me. The next day, when I was sober, he asked if I'd skip night school and go to a concert with him. I immediately had a bad feeling. I knew I shouldn't go. I didn't go.

Another time I was at a party, hanging out with a bunch of friends when one guy was getting extra friendly with me. He picked me up and carried me to a bedroom and closed the door. I knew immediately what was about to happen if I didn't fight like hell. I fought like hell.

Another time I had been dating a guy for a while. I truly loved and cared for him and wanted to keep dating him. I woke up one morning with a distinct impression that I needed to end things with him asap. I clearly knew that he was into things I didn't want to be involved with. I broke up with him.

How did I know any of those things? This wasn't previously thought-out knowledge. This information did not present itself after concerted effort in meditation. This wasn't even an answer to any question that had previously crossed my mind. This was immediate knowledge deep in my gut.

I thank God every day that this part of me has always been alive and alert. I trust this knowledge above and beyond, without a doubt, no matter what. I listen, and I do. I feel like any incredible or powerful person could stand in front of me and proclaim, "This person is safe." and if it came between listening to them or trusting my gut, I'd go with my gut to be safe. Maybe that isn't right. Maybe I have an extra dose of fear. Maybe all the karate lessons as a kid have me hypersensitive. Or maybe, just maybe, it is God watching over me. Whatever it is, I don't want to go through life without it.

This type of information has come on less sensitive topics. I had two campuses to choose from for my massage school. I knew which one was right and went with my gut. It was absolutely the right environment for me.

I had multiple job offers in Vegas. I was desperate for a job, but they didn't feel right. I turned them down. My dream job was offered next.

I had two babies and always thought I would have more. My intuition knows this isn't the right time and that these two might be my only babies. As unpopular as the decision may be for extended family, and even though it wasn't what I expected either, I'm sticking with my gut.

I am so thankful that in each of these experiences, especially in the first three, that I did not hesitate. I didn't question it. I didn't feel guilty, and I did not care what anyone else may have thought of my decision. I don't know why that is. I don't know how to teach that to you. I only want to wake you up to this gift inside of you.

Have you ever had an experience where you KNEW deep in your gut what to do? The knowledge was clear, and it was instant. Did you follow through? What happened or didn't happen because of it? In certain instances, you may never know the outcome for following through with an impression. Some are worth never knowing if they kept you safe.

Our intuition is vital in going about this life as safely as we can. Sometimes there will be absolutely no rhyme or reason as to why you have a sudden instinct to do something. I encourage you to trust it. Each new experience in trusting your intuition will strengthen your faith in this part of you.

So how do you know the difference between just a thought and your intuition? *You'll feel it in your gut.* It won't be in your head. It won't be wishy-washy and like the chatty teenager that typically hangs out up there freaked out all the time. If it had a voice, it would have a deep, powerful, God-like feel to it.

It is typically a distinct impression that seems to hit you like a ton of bricks (if keeping you safe) or with clear, precise information that doesn't budge. You won't be able to talk yourself out of the pit in your stomach. It will remain until it is heard and honored. You can clearly tell it isn't your own thought because, oftentimes, you won't see it coming, or you may have been heading in the opposite direction entirely. All three of those boys I enjoyed being around. I would have gone. I would have stayed.

Practice noticing these impressions. This isn't to say that you seek out or try to have these impressions. That will only confuse you, I promise. You don't prepare for them; you simply go about your life. The large impressions are few and far between, so don't hold your breath for those. What you will notice, however, is that there are surprisingly small impressions that happen more frequently than you realize. When you follow through, you'll be glad. Like the impression to stop and get gas before work only to realize later, when something urgent came up, you needed that full tank. Or the impression to pick up some extra milk while at the grocery store only to get home later to a sick wife who has run out of milk for the baby. These little things happen all the time. Practice noticing them and following through.

Stick with the impressions you have. They may only come once, like the first time you shake hands with your neighbor and have the impression, "*Don't let your kids be around him alone.*" Are you willing to trust that feeling months or years down the road? What if no one else agrees? What if you're really wanting to go out with your friends and his wife has offered to babysit? You need to be in tune enough with yourself to trust your gut and stick with it no matter what, no matter who thinks you're crazy. Be strong. Be brave. That guy who gives you the heebies, but won't stop asking you out? What do you do when he offers to take you to your favorite concert? Do you cave then? This isn't to say that every situation will end terribly. Some things are just not for you, like a job you felt you shouldn't take. You won't be able to explain it, but I hope that you stick with it.

One final note: I want you to know that if you have been blindsided by something with no warning from your "gut", that it is not your fault. There is no fault for that. Some things we are meant to experience, and you may not know why. Trust that there was a reason for each experience in your life. It is what it is, and you are not responsible. Let your previous experiences be in the hands of God.

If you have experienced warnings and didn't follow through and something negative resulted from it, *please refrain from beating yourself up for that!* It is okay. I have plenty of those experiences too. Let that be a building block in your knowledge and experiences. Let it strengthen your faith in your ability to trust your gut in the future.

There is a man that I look up to very much. He was the prophet of the church I belonged to and recently passed away. Years ago, he shared a story of being in a meeting and having a distinct impression to get up and go visit a friend who was in the hospital. He didn't want to be rude to those in the meeting and seem disrespectful for leaving. The speaker was almost done, so even though the impression was strong and direct, he decided to wait until the talk was over. He then left as quickly as he could, running out the door even before the closing prayer. As he ran through the corridors of the hospital there was a commotion outside this friend's room, and a nurse stopped him outside the door.

She asked, "Are you Bishop Monson?" After affirming, the nurse said, "I'm sorry. The patient was calling your name just before he died." Fighting back the tears, he turned and walked back into the night. He vowed then and there that he would never again fail to act upon a prompting from the Lord. He would acknowledge the impressions of the Spirit when they came, and he would follow wherever they led him.[60]

We all make mistakes. If you have, know that everyone has. Remember, today is a new day. Choose to trust those impressions to the best of your abilities from here on out.

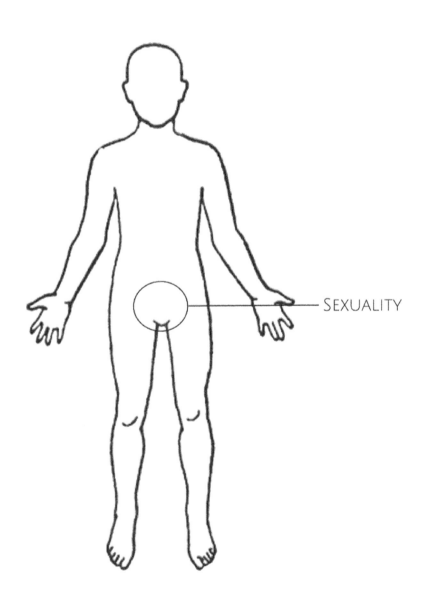

SEXUALITY

14

SEXUALITY

I hate the circle on this graph here for two reasons. One, our sexuality includes more than these parts (just saying). If I drew the circle correctly, it would be more like the personal space bubble, only much larger! And two, because it's an awkward circle on the poor figure's genitals. But for the sake of simplicity, I'm sticking with it y'all. Let's do this!

Okay, do you remember how I told you that the original list of our pieces was different? This was something not on their list. I remember standing in my kitchen pondering this book and what it is I believe makes up who we are. I couldn't shake the feeling that I needed to include sexuality. The sheer terror coming over me with that thought made me even more sure that I needed to include it. The fact that this can be such a hard topic to discuss is probably proof that we need to talk about it more. So I'm going to be brave.

Here is why I was terrified: The statistics of abuse, human trafficking, pornography, and sexually related addictions are heart-wrenching. There are a lot of people in pain and trying to heal from traumatic experiences or addictions. Along with these issues, I know there are many suffering from confusion, shame, guilt, etc. about their own gender and sexuality. Couple this with the fact that it's not a topic most people are willing to chat about, and there is a lot of buried pain that is left unhealed for far too long. It all breaks my heart. If you are struggling to feel connected with yourself, if you're struggling to feel safe and comfortable inside of your skin, If the topic of sexuality, in general, makes you squirm and want to skip to the next chapter, I want to encourage you to stick this one out with me! Allow yourself to be a little uncomfortable, and please stay. This is an important part of us. It's an important part of our mental, emotional, and physical health. It's an important part of our relationships both to ourselves and others, and it is an important part of your spirituality—which I'm going to help you understand if you'll stick around.

First and foremost, I want you to know that I see you. I am here with you. My heart wants to burst open wide with love for all of you. Whatever it is that you may have been through, or might be struggling with, I want you to know again that healing is possible. It is just as possible for you to heal and thrive in this area of your life as it is in any other.

I'll admit, I wish I had a magic wand that could heal the whole world. But I know that even if such a thing existed, to take away difficulty in your life would also take away a gift that you might not be able to gain in any other way. Whatever you might be experiencing, may very well turn into your greatest strength one day. So instead, all I can do is sit and hold space for you as you grow into this sacred capacity within you.

There are a few profound lessons I've been learning about our sexuality, and these are the things that I feel inclined to share right now. The first is that no matter what you have been through or what you've been told or how shameful sex seems to you—*your sexuality is a gift, and a good thing.*

Our sexuality was given to us to be a beautiful part of our lives. It is one of the most powerful ways that we can connect with ourselves and each other. This intensity is what can make it an incredibly healing and sacred experience for our minds, bodies, and souls.

Because it is a powerful way to connect with others, it can be equally as harmful if used incorrectly. But Dr. Jennifer Finlayson-Fife explains it perfectly: "It is not sexuality that corrupts people, it's people that corrupt sexuality."[61]

Your sexuality was inherently intended to be a blessing and a strength to you, a life-giving source, and a living well to draw from, a *gift,* and a *good thing.*

All of us are inherently sensual beings by nature—all of us. We were literally created from the act of it, and it is how we further the human family. We are drawn to it for a reason, and there is nothing wrong with that. Let me repeat that in another form—there is nothing wrong with *you.* Your desires, no matter how weird you might feel about them, can teach you a great deal about yourself. They can also teach you a great deal about your connection to God if you let them. So please give yourself space to relax, and trust that you feel the way you do for a reason.

I personally was raised in a culture where sexuality was shamed, hushed, and sometimes worse—ignored. I thank God that I was raised in a home where my parents didn't give in to that too much. We talk and joke about sex, and I'm glad. But I can say that I still grew up more aware of the dark or shameful side of sex. There seemed to be warnings and danger signs about it at church and in my community. I spent most of my childhood and teen years terrified of my own body and terrified of boys. I was under the impression that at any given moment, a boy (or we) could "lose control" and the results of that could completely "destroy my life forever." Obviously, that was not the healthiest of ideas. I see now how wrong that messaging was and how those thoughts crippled me. I also can't deny that these beliefs instilled fear into my relationships and the way I've lived my life.

There seems to be a lot of shame-based beliefs sur-rounding very healthy and normal desires. When there is a heightened amount of shame, usually we will do one of two things: We will do our best to shut it off completely, or we will overindulge in unhealthy ways. Shame creates this high contrast of extremes, neither of which are healthy for us. It is just as detrimental to our happiness and full expression of life to shut off sexually as it is to over-indulge. If what you are seeking is a joyful life, you will be finding it somewhere in a healthy middle ground where you neither deny your body and soul nor overindulge in harmful ways.

Your life is ultimately yours to live, and you will have to decide what choices you will make and when. Choosing consciously when, where, how, and who you connect with will be best if it brings your soul peace and joy.

So what does it look like to be healthy? In my opin-ion, healthy sexuality should grant you and your partner a sacred space where both people choose to share this part of themselves with the other. Both should feel safe, seen, heard, and cared for. It is to foster love and intimacy not only behind closed doors but throughout the entire relationship. It is to allow each of you room to grow, laugh, play, and connect.

Healthy sexuality is to embrace with open hearts and minds this god-given gift in a way that honors your highest selves. It is to lift each other up to higher ground.

In order to do this, to truly share yourself with another person, you need to know another very important thing. *Your body belongs to you.*

One thing I think that really stood in my way of getting to this place of feeling safe and comfortable sexually is the sense of belonging to myself instead of belonging to another human being.

It is a unique experience to be a religious girl who mostly follows all the "rules". Because essentially we are taught to deny ourselves anything that sparks sexual feelings until we are married. After this, we sign a couple of papers and anything goes as long as we're together! I went from entirely disconnecting or shaming any sexual feelings at all, to one day being "allowed" to do whatever I wanted to do. Only now it was not solely allowed, but expected. All of the sudden there was this new man in the room with whom I made a deal with and he was the one who made my sexuality legitimate. The whole thing felt a little surreal and while it was a lot of fun to figure it out, I still felt that my body didn't belong to me, it belonged to someone else…

I lived for years feeling disconnected—like my body was not created for me, but for everyone around me. It was an incubator for growing babies, a source of food for them once they were born, a playground for toddlers, and a source of comfort for my husband when he needed it. It needed to look pretty, act pretty, sound pretty, and smell pretty for everyone around me. My body was a separate entity from me and I made sure she fit the part at all costs. It seemed that most of my identity and self-worth was wrapped up in how well she fulfilled these roles and yet, I felt like I hardly knew her.

All of this changed for me one night in the middle of the night. My husband and I had recently moved. There were changes in our plans of where we were going to be living and we were in a temporary home for the limbo. While I am used to moving (this was my 31st move since I had left my parent's house at age 15.) The longings for a steady place to live were especially strong in me this night as I fell asleep. My heart ached for a home.

I laid awake for a long while until I finally drifted off to sleep. In the middle of the night, I woke up to a whisper in my mind that startled me.

"Your body is your home." the voice said. "Your body is your home."

This one sentence continued repeating in my mind, slowly waking me up until my eyes opened. I sat there in bed that night, eyes wide open, soaking up this heavenly message with tears rolling down my cheeks. My mind then opened up revealing to me that this search I have been on for most of my life was not a search for an actual home, but a *longing to come back home to myself.* My ability to abandon places, people, and things was a direct reflection of my inner ability to abandon myself—to run away from who I am and what I wanted. *To run away from home.* I sobbed that night with a deep inner knowing that I *was* home. That I have always been home.

The next morning I woke up and sat in meditation. I envisioned myself inside of my body—inside of my new home. I placed my hand on my heart, touching myself as if it were for the first time. I imagined my body was an actual home. I walked through the hallways, examined all the floors and doors. I slowly checked every room, touching every piece of old furniture. As I walked through this home I felt equally as if I had been meeting her for the first time, and as if I had known her my whole life. She seemed to be able to speak to me. I recognized that she had been waiting for me to come back to her—patiently awaiting my return.

I promised her I was here to stay, that I was sorry I ever left. I told her I was going to care for her fiercely this time. As I looked around it seemed as if someone else had been living there and I told her I would be taking back all of the keys. I called upon everyone in my life whom I had given away a "key" or who had taken a key without my permission. I asked for my keys back. I told them that they are welcome to come and visit, but that the keys belong to me now. *I reclaimed my body back.* I awoke from that meditation a very different person than I was the night before and have never been the same since. *I have finally come back home.*

In order for you to share yourself fully and completely with any other person, it will be very important for you to know deep within your soul that you belong to you first. Your body is yours, not theirs. Your heart is yours, not theirs. Your soul is yours, not theirs. For true love to be true love, both people need to own their own bodies and respect the others'. Your body is your home. Theirs is theirs. Unlike physical homes that you might decide to share only one of, this home will not be shared. Visited maybe, but not shared. You both deserve to hold and own the keys to your own bodies. Always. *Your body belongs to you. Your body is your home.*

My last and final thought I have for this chapter is the one I promised to explain earlier. That is, *your sexuality is directly related to your spirituality.*

This concept might be an entirely new concept for you, especially those who have had a lot of shame surrounding sex, so try to have an open mind. Be patient with me and yourself on this one.

There is something that happens when we travel into such a vulnerable and instinctual place physically. We also travel to a more sacred place within our souls, a place where our ego can shut off, and we can feel and see things that connect us to our higher selves and our higher purpose.

You long for things while you're in this state of mind, whether it be playfulness, spontaneity, purity, safety, deep passion, etc. Before jumping the gun and shaming yourself like crazy for whatever random desires emerge within you. I want you to stop and take a moment to get to know what they are. Most likely the very thing you long for in-between the sheets is the very thing your soul is longing for spiritually speaking.[62] Wild, I know. It is absolutely amazing what you can learn when you stop judging yourself.

Just as we are drawn to certain qualities in a mate, we are drawn to specific experiences. The qualities you admire in a mate are usually the same qualities you long to awaken or develop within yourself. The sexual experiences you desire to have contain a similar spiritual message. While not everything you dream up is meant to be experienced sexually, you can learn a great deal from the message.

Take a moment to be brutally honest with yourself. What is it you are longing for? Newness? Excitement? Respect? Do you long to be known entirely? Or completely consumed in love? If so, there is a very high chance that your soul is longing to be known spiritually by God—completely consumed in His love. Do you long for purity or safety? Most likely you are spiritually longing to be pure and safe. Do you long for playfulness or spontaneity? Most likely your soul is feeling bogged down spiritually, and you need the freedom to lighten up or explore. Do you enjoy the mysterious or unknown? Spiritually speaking your soul might have pieces that are unknown or hidden that might be ready to be explored. If you can relax and get to know yourself in this way, you can start to honor your soul's deepest desires in all areas of your life, not only this one. These messages from your spirit can help you find your God-given path and true nature.

To understand this connection to your spirituality is to create a life-giving well for you to draw endless spiritual knowledge from. Your sexual side can be this sacred place you visit that connects you both to the heavens and your higher self. This is what it is to practice sacred sexuality.

If that takes you time to grasp, it's okay. I'm still learning as well. For now, let's move on to healing practices...

Healing practices to adopt:

1. **Stop shaming yourself for your sexual desire.**
   Remember, God gave it to you. Your sexuality is a gift and a good thing. Allow yourself to define what is good and right for you. Something this sacred is allowed to be determined by yourself and your God (not the

'Gods' who stand at pulpits, the God who speaks directly to you.) Let it be sacred and between the two of you without worry. Do your best to drown out the shameful messages around you on this topic and give yourself a little grace! You don't have to have it all figured out. That is the whole point of life. You get to learn and grow at your own pace and your own speed. You know your heart. You'll know what is right for you. Trust yourself and set yourself free to make choices that honor your highest self and the highest in others.

2. **Come back home to yourself.**

   I created a guided meditation similar to the one I did the day I woke up to the voice in the night. In this meditation, you will come back home to yourself and take back the "keys" to your home. You can find it on my site www.heatherfalter.com.[63]

3. **Start noticing your desires.**

   What are you drawn to? What excites you? What do you long for? What stirs emotion in you? What makes your heart skip a beat?

   When you recognize those things, instead of getting flustered, being overcome with shame, or trying to shut it off—notice what it is and then what characteristics it has. Maybe it is strength, maybe it is gentleness, maybe it is respect, maybe it is a sense of security. Notice that the qualities you long for are qualities your soul wants to become. It is not someone else you are seeking. It is yourself.

4. **Take the message from your desires and start developing these qualities.**

   Write down what you learn. Continue to follow your heart and recognize that *while not everything is meant to be explored sexually, there is a reason you feel the way you feel.* **Take the message** from these desires and develop those qualities you are drawn to. Incorporate these healthy ideals into the remainder of your life.

5. **Begin to see every other person's body as their home.**

Every living soul deserves the same respect that you do, that is, to feel safe and secure in their own skin. Every living soul has the right to say what happens to their "home." It doesn't matter who this person is or how closely you are connected to them—their body is theirs, not yours. Teach them this concept through the respect you show them. There is no one too young to learn this. Teach your children young. Let them decide who they will hug, kiss, or let hold them. Give them the voice they deserve. Teach them that they belong to themselves, and they get to decide what they feel safe and comfortable with. Show your mate through your example that their body is sacred. Treat it as such in all of your encounters together and watch as your relationship blooms.

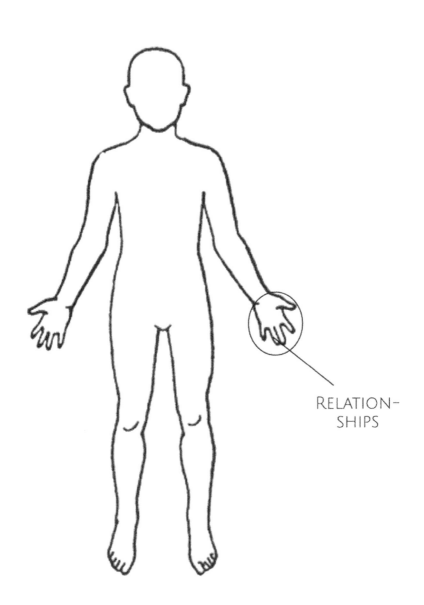

RELATION-
SHIPS

15

RELATIONSHIPS

I f you could think of the top 5 most important people in your life, who would they be? Feel free to write them down if you would like. Otherwise, take mental note of them in order. Now, If you could give a quick answer as to how these relationships are going right now, what would you say? Do you feel good about the state of your relationships?

What if you extend your reach to the top 10 or the top 20 people in your life? How are those relationships doing? Just take a moment to reflect. Do you get along with the most important people in your life? How are things going in your relationship with your significant other? Your kids? Your mom and dad? Your siblings? Your boss? Don't worry. If you wish some of them were going a little better, that's okay. They will be!

The nice thing about relationships is they are moldable, pliable, and they can be nourished. Just like a sick or dying plant, they can be brought back to vibrant health. This process can be surprisingly quick and simple.

Before I tell you what works, I need to tell you what does NOT work. This unfortunately is the most common way most of us approach mending a relationship. I approached my relationships in this way for years and it was exhausting! This is what I would do: If I felt like someone was upset with me, I would hyper-focus on that relationship. I would think of all the kind things I could do for them and I would give and give of myself endlessly until they liked me again! Sounds legit right? If you're nodding your head yes, you're a giver like me and probably place your sense of self-worth in the opinions of others. Now don't get me wrong, I don't think there is anything wrong with being a generous giver—until, UNTIL, you are giving so much of yourself that you have nothing left, OR until you are giving of yourself in a way that sacrifices your own identity, OR until you are giving in order to change the way someone feels about you. These things seem innocent, but I promise you they are harmful to the relationship and are robbing you of a deeper love.

My approach to relationships has changed dramatically as I've grown older. Thank goodness! My newer approach is much more effective, healthy, and fulfilling for everyone involved. It involves a few key points that seem counter-intuitive, so stick with me on these. These lessons learned are also my healing practices to adopt. Here we go!

1. **I focus on myself.** (Gasp!)

   The idea of focusing on myself, caring about my own needs, and making myself a priority used to feel like a 4-letter word. I'm not joking. Now I know that meeting my own needs are the *first* needs that need to be met. They are. We cannot draw water from an empty well, and it took running my well nearly dry to realize that an empty wife, mother, and daughter was a rip not only on me but everyone who was in a relationship with me. Those who knew me were not getting 'me' at all. They were getting a hollow, empty, tired, strung-out and watered down replica of me. No one felt entirely happy when I was this way.

I had to learn to figuratively (and literally) sit down at the table and serve myself 'biscuits and gravy' along with everybody else. I joined the ranks of those in the household getting fed. I made sure my own needs were being met either equally or if someone needs to go first (like the placing of oxygen masks on a plummeting airplane) I make sure to place mine first. (Gasp again!) How did I not get this before? This makes sense to you, right? You meet your own needs first, and then with your fresh air, beating heart, and fully functioning brain, you help your children, your husband, your neighbor, and their friend's dog get their oxygen masks on as well.

There is another reason I focus on myself when my relationships are struggling. I have learned that my relationships are a direct reflection of the relationship I have within. Whatever I'm struggling with in some-one else, usually has powerful internal messages for me. The things I'm rejecting in them are the things I'm rejecting in me. For example, my kiddos have been running wild lately. They have had so much freedom this summer running around and doing whatever they want with their friends! It's been on my nerves. Before reacting to them I've learned to lower my guard and ask *why* this is getting to me. I've realized that while, yes it would be nice to reign them in a little bit, I'm also rejecting their freedom because I'm rejecting my own right now! My face is stuck in my computer and I hav-en't given myself the freedom to run around, let loose and play. I'm not caring for my basic need for free time and adventure. Ironically the remedy is not to demand they come in the house and do chores, the remedy is to join them! The remedy is to shut my computer off and play! It is almost comical how often the answer to a healthier happier relationship is almost the exact opposite of what I instinctually wanted to do. And this leads me to my next point.

2. **I let people be who they are.**

This is one of my favorite ways to release tension in my relationships. Sometimes I need the reminder, so if you need it too, here it is: *We are different on purpose, and it is a beautiful thing!* Let the people in your life be who they are, and not only who they are but where they are at. Let them do what they're doing.

We all go through our own life lessons. Let the people in your life go through theirs without your disapproving eye twitching at them! Just let them be. One of my favorite pieces of advice before marrying my husband was to not worry about where he is at and what he is doing. The advice was specifically toward spiritual things. My council was to, "*Keep your eyes on God and make your way toward Him. Don't worry about the other person. You keep moving forward yourself, and things will work out.*"[64]

Like Mother Theresa said, his life is between Him and God. As long as he is not harming us and he's taking care of the basics, WHO CARES?! We think if we are not watching people and telling them how to live their lives, they will fall apart. This is not so. The exact opposite is true. The things you want for other people are probably things they want for themselves too. Forcing it upon them will only drive them further from it and further from you. Let them be and watch as they find the path that is right for them.

3. **I let people dislike me!** (Whaaaat?)

I know it's foreign. At least it was to younger me. I don't know if I got too old, too tired to care, or too happy inside of my own skin, but what other people think of me has become less and less interesting lately. I realized one day that pretending to be someone I'm not for someone else was a waste of my life. I hit this point where I realized that It was time. I had to be myself. In doing so, I would give the people around me the freedom to decide whether they liked me or not, and I am learning to be OK with their opinions either way as long as I get to be who I am. This 'coming home' to myself—that I talked about in the previous chapter—is a big contributing factor to the peace that I feel on the matter. The more I have learned to love myself and fulfill my own needs, the less it has mattered who is by my side. Everyone else is a beautiful bonus to an already beautiful life, so it's OK if I'm not someone's cup of tea! The people who are meant to be with me *will be*. The ones who are no *will not*. I have learned to let relationships go that have run their course, and I have become more comfortable letting people dislike me.

4. **I learned that any long-term relationship is going to get messy.**

   That is exactly what love is supposed to do. Didn't you know?! We grew up thinking our partner's existence was going to fulfill us. In reality, we find out that the relationship is really meant to purge us of our crappy behaviors while we learn to fulfill ourselves! Life is funny like that.

   I learned that there are stages to love. The first two, falling in love and becoming a couple, are really great. What I didn't know is that every relationship will hit stage three—the point where issues come up.

   Most people will end their relationship in this stage, convinced that it was a mistake to begin with. What they don't know is that this stage will continue to appear in every future relationship. Stage three is a gift, meant to purge both people of their unhealthy ways.

   Any close relationship will push your buttons, stress you out, and make you want to run away at times! If you choose to stay, you'll have to find another way out of the pain, which is releasing and resolving your issues together, being vulnerable, and working through the ugly stuff. If a couple can make it through this stage without throwing in the towel or giving into complacency, they will make it through to a connection that exceeds what they previously had. They move on to the final two stages: real and lasting love, and a love that can make a difference in this world with the power of two.[65]

If issues come up in a relationship, I show up to the mess willing to clean it up. I am willing to be honest, admit my faults, change, and forgive. Relationships get messy. It's fine! If I am met with a partner who is willing to do the dirty work with me, I know that the mess is worth cleaning, and what we'll create is far better than where we once were.

5. **I learned that the other person's actions are not a prerequisite for my kindness.**

Last night I was sitting at the dinner table with my husband. He asked how my book was going, and I told him I was in the chapter on relationships. I asked him what advice I should give. True to his simple nature, he said, "Uh...be kind." End of sermon! Except this is only the end of his word sermon. His actual display of kindness is endless! His kindness is the reason I married him. After eight years, I can honestly say he has been kind most of the time.

For Travis, his kindness doesn't change if people aren't kind to him. It just is because *he* is. Very, *very* rarely does the man get upset. I've only seen it a few times, and he is quick to seek out forgiveness when he does. Our relationship isn't perfect. Of course, we still have occasional disagreements and different points of view, but through it all, he continues to listen when I talk, looks me in my eyes, and is gentle throughout tough conversations. Luckily, we both have the same respect for each other, but there have been plenty of people who have come and gone who didn't respect him. People have taken advantage of him, talked negatively about him and to him, and he has *continued to show them kindness anyway.* A lot of people might not know what to do with that, but that is simply who he is. He isn't looking for attention. He isn't looking to be the "better man." (In fact, this might be the most uncomfortable part of my book for him to read.) He simply is kind to people.

Being married to him has stretched me because, honestly, I'm not so quick to let things roll off my back when my feelings are hurt. But, for him and his peaceful nature, he doesn't like to let it cramp his style. He continues to be an example to me that *other people's actions are not a prerequisite for our kindness.* They can say, do, and think whatever they want. They can even hate us, and we can still be nice. That doesn't mean you have to keep negative people in your life. It only means that you continue to be a good person no matter what. Mother Theresa understood this and said it perfectly:

"People are often unreasonable, irrational, and self-centered.
Forgive them anyway.
If you are kind, people may accuse you of selfish, ulterior motives.
Be kind anyway.
If you are successful, you will win some unfaithful friends and some genuine enemies.
Succeed anyway.
If you are honest and sincere, people may deceive you.
Be honest and sincere anyway.
What you spend years creating, others could destroy overnight.
Create anyway.
If you find serenity and happiness, some may be jealous.
Be happy anyway.
The good you do today, will often be forgotten.

Do good anyway.
Give the best you have, and it will never be enough.
Give your best anyway.
In the final analysis, it is between you and God
It was never between you and them anyway."[66]

6. **I learned that I am neither more important or less important than any other person. Any. Other. Person.**

We are a human family; meaning we are all equally loved and cherished by our Heavenly Parents. I don't care who you are or what you've done. You don't matter more or less than anyone else. If you are trying to be someone more important, more significant, more loved than the person next to you, your relationships are probably suffering. I only know because I have been there. I know that might put your stomach in knots, the idea that the person next to you is as valuable as you, but please hear me out. This will heal a huge part of your heart if you let it. We are not as different as we appear.

When I leave my local Wal-Mart and see the drug—addict bum on the corner, I see someone different than who I saw as a young child. I used to see a bum who looked sick and who I felt sorry for, but not in a nice way—a pitiful way. Now, do you know what I see? I see me; only one day I picked up a book instead of something stronger to ease my pain.

When I am in a grocery store and see a refugee mother scrambling to contain her babies in the check out line, do you know what I see? I see me—a mother terrified for the future of her children. Only I'm somewhere where I can speak the common language, and I feel comfortable calling it my home. And then I wonder why in the hell I was born in this free country instead of her.

When I am at the movies and spot two gay guys holding hands, do you know what I see? I see me;

someone who loves someone else and is trying to follow their heart. The only difference is I am attracted to someone of the opposite sex, making my relationship much more acceptable by the public eye than theirs.

When I am sitting in church and spot the transgender person who is sitting alone on the back row, do you know what I see? I see me; a person in search of finding herself; a person willing to be hated and experience extreme loneliness in hopes for a glimpse of God's love. I also see my teenage self wanting more than anything to know if someone up there could see me, hoping love could find me on the back pew, even with traces of alcohol on my breath. Then I wonder, "How come when I was young and learned of my gender, I felt good, and this person felt something was wrong? Why do I feel that and she doesn't?"

On the flip side, when I attend concerts and see a person totally in their element, belting out their talents on a stage, do you know what I see then? I also see me; someone who has talents inside that might be admired by millions one day if I keep believing. I feel happy for them and proud of their talent as if they were my own. Do you know what else I end up doing when I'm at a big show? I look around and notice all the people totally jamming out next to me. I wonder about them. If they were on that stage giving it their all, what would they be doing? And would I be just as strongly tempted to worship them as well if they stepped into their own?

You see, we are all equal. You being human makes you just as vulnerable to sin and just as worthy of accomplishment as the next person. That person in your life who you continue to think is less than you, they're not. Oftentimes the difference between two totally different lives was a sliver; a moment of weakness versus a moment of courage, or simply being born in a different home that ultimately takes you worlds apart.

You could be them. *In fact, you very well would be them had you been born and raised under their circumstances and given the same brain to work with.*

Remember that in the end, you will leave this world the way you came. No matter how accomplished your life was here, you will stand before your Maker one day, probably in very regular clothing, and talk about things as simple as how kind you were to the people around you. When you go about your life remembering this, you will see people in a new light. Your wife, your kids, your employees, your boss, and even the janitor at your local hospital will become just as amazing to you as, say, Beyoncé.

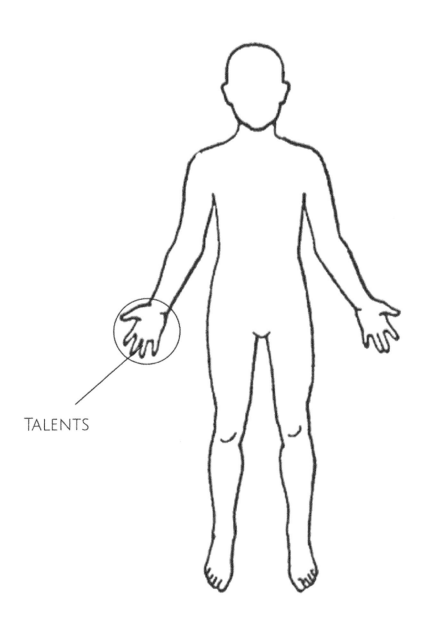

TALENTS

16

TALENTS

have a confession to make. This book has been finished for months, and I have not done a single thing with it. It's been entirely edited, sent back ready-to-go, and I have let it sit in my computer—haunting me like a bad dream that won't go away. I have literally pleaded with God multiple times to "Call someone else." and I have muttered the words "I can't do this." under my breath more times than I can count.

If you follow my blog, you know I've been promising this book for over a year now.[67] I also have a website being built for a company that doesn't even exist because this book is still sitting in my computer!

I have another confession to make. I obviously had an entirely different beginning to this chapter. It was full of fluff and all sorts of hollow encouragement about developing your talents with quotes that we've all heard, but here's the honest truth. Sharing your talents may very well make you feel like you are both going to vomit and shit your pants at the exact same time!

It will.

It doesn't matter what your gift is. Once you find it you'll be faced with all sorts of opposition. Do you want to know why? Because your gift can change the world. That's why.

Because people need it. That's why. Because you were destined to figure it out, conquer all odds and grow into an incredibly powerful force for good. That's why.

If there is one thing I've learned as I've been hovering my imaginary pointer finger over the 'delete key' of this entire text—it is this: *The longing to share my gift isn't going anywhere.* There is no 'delete key' to knowing deep down who we are and what we're meant to do here.

I could back down. I could listen to and follow my fears. I could waste more precious time. But where does that leave me? Exactly where I was when I picked up this little laptop to begin with. Only this time with a solidified conviction that I don't have what it takes. But I KNOW that even if I give up now, the desire I have to write this book is *not going to go away.*

So, It's midnight. I'm sitting in my dark kitchen with a choice to make. Am I going to leave this book in my computer, left unseen, unheard, and unread—left to rot and die in a minefield of other wasted dreams? Or am I going to stare my fear in the face, and send this book off to a publishing company and move forward?

This is what it comes down to, my friend. A decision to make. And for some reason, we have this idea that we'll accomplish great things with ease, but as I spoke to a friend recently about my fears, she wisely responded, "One thing I have learned about fear. We think we will act when the fear is gone, but we need to act while our knees are shaking."[68] Oh, how I needed her timely advice.

If you're holding this book in your hands, I acted while my knees were still shaking.

Also, If you're reading this, I am here to tell you that the longings that *you* have arent going to go away. They will continue to press you until you act on them in faith; until you take what is a hopeful fancy and make it a reality.

I'm also here to tell you that you're worth it. YOU are the reason I'm here writing this. Because I wanted to tell you, not just through my words, but through my very actions, that your dreams are just as special as mine, and they are just as worthy of sharing.

You have talents, my friend—a lot of them. You know what they are. Even if you don't *know* that you *know* what they are. There is a longing inside of you that has been asking you to stand up, step up, and take up space here on earth that only you can fill.

I hope you fill it.

So, now that I've altered the flow, the tone, and the entire beginning to this chapter, I feel tempted to rewrite the rest, but here's the thing. This girl has got to move forward! So I'm going to leave the rest of the chapter here for you, unedited and choppy as it may be because I think it's still valid, and I think you have it in you to forgive me!

"If you take any activity, any art, any discipline, any skill
- take it and push it as far as it will go, push it beyond
where it has ever been before, push it to the wildest
edges of edges, then you force it into the realm of magic."

-Rhonda Byrne, The Magic[69]

You were born with genius in you. You are naturally inclined to certain things that make you special. You also have things that you are drawn to that can become talents if you spent time with them. You love things. You love, love, love them. Are you doing them?

It is never going to be easy. There is never a time where you are ready. Going for your dream is going to make you want to vomit and cry and run and hide. Believe me, I know!

I hope you do them anyway. I hope you find a way. I hope you turn to the person you love and say, "Honey, this is all I've ever wanted. This is what I want to do." And I hope they support you. If not, I hope you find a way anyway. Here's the thing—at the end of your life it will be YOU with regret, not them. It's not on them. It's your dream, your passion, your love. It is your job to go for it. They may not understand, but *other people's understanding is not a prerequisite for you living your best life.*

If you are going to do anything with your life, anything for a living, I hope you choose to do something that you naturally are drawn to; something you are good at, and that brings you joy. *Success is not the same without giving your gift.*

Both of my little brothers (shout out! Oh heeey!), BOTH of my little brothers skydive for a living. THEY SKYDIVE FOR A LIVING, Y'ALL! *Don't tell me you can't do what you love for a living.*

My mom lost her house, her husband, and a lot of her kids left home all within a short time. She was bankrupt, with no formal degree and at the lowest points in her life. She started her own business and now does really well financially. She is one of my greatest examples of grit and persistence. She has, against all odds, created a life that is true to herself, with lots of travel, swimming, sundresses, and sunshine. *Don't tell me that it's impossible, or that now is not the right time.*

There is no right time. You have to decide to do it and then do it. God loves this stuff and will be all over opening the right doors for you. Miracles will happen. No one roots harder for you than God and His angels who know the power of your gift. They send you little signs all the time. They send shivers up your spine and the aching in your heart when you see someone else doing the very thing you want to do. There is a way for you to do it. If you'll get up and start moving, they will show you the way.

I once heard that God will have two questions for you when you die.

First, *"How well did you love?"* (beginning with a spouse, your kids, extended family, friends, etc., in that order). And second, (this one floored me when I heard it), *"What did you do with your talents?"*[70] Whether that is true or not, whether He or She or whoever is up there asks me that or not—I know dang well I will be there asking myself the same question. "Heather, what did you do with your talents?" I want to say to myself, *"I used them all up. Every ounce I could give, I gave. I gave with my whole heart no matter how vulnerable and awkward and undeveloped I may have been. I worked hard, and I gave them. I searched them out, and I gave them again."*

One of the most important turning points for me in 'becoming whole' and becoming more of myself was seeking out the talents God has blessed me with and devoting time to developing them. I've worked hard to train my mind to automatically assume that if anyone else can do something, I can too. I've consciously made the effort to spend less time mindlessly scrolling the internet and more time practicing things that I love and am naturally drawn to. As I've done these things, I've noticed how much happier I am. Developing these talents has brought peace and joy into my life. They have also opened doors I never dreamed of!

The cover of this book was a painting I painted for myself one night. I had no intention of showing it to anyone ever. I was having a hard time and couldn't explain it. I needed help understanding what I was feeling and decided to do a little painting to see if I could paint what I was feeling. This painting still means everything to me. It was the beginning of my promise to find and pick up whatever was broken within me and to step back into the light. This painting that started out as a simple journal entry holds the potential to become an entire business; a business where I will dedicate my life to helping others pick up their broken pieces.

I can't imagine a life without developing talents and sharing them. It is literally the happiest, best, and most favorite thing I do. Not because I love the spotlight (believe me, that part is borderline excruciating), but because nothing compares to handing someone a gift and seeing it touch their heart. I can't count how many times I have stood still and watched someone weep over a gift I've placed in their hands. I know those gifts weren't actually from me. They were from God, and I was only the deliverer. Still, nothing, nothing, nothing brings me more joy than this.

I know our gifts are from God, all of ours. They were meant to be used, worn out, shared, and exhausted—not only in their prime after the gift was mastered but in every stage from infancy to maturity—all along the way with anyone we can reach. You never know who needs your gift. You will not know until the gift has been given, and even still, you may never know how you have helped.

So what about you? What things are you naturally drawn to? What do you enjoy doing? Sometimes these things are hidden. Sometimes they have been gifted, but not yet received. Sometimes it takes an open mind and a little bit of fun exploring new things to find out what you enjoy. You'll know you've hit a sweet spot when it's something you love and something that can bless others' lives if you share it. That sweet spot can become your life's work.

I love the quote by Steve Jobs that says:

"Your work is going to fill a large part of your life, and the only way to be truly satisfied is to do what you believe is great work. And the only way to do great work is to love what you do. If you haven't found it yet, keep looking and don't settle."[71]

God gave you talents. YOU reading this, my friend, are not exempt. When God created you, He gifted you with talents to develop. Have you found them? Do you use them? Have you shared them with the rest of us? You did not come here to remain hidden and small. I know it's scary, but you did not come here to ride life out in the shadows, afraid of your own spotlight. You were created to shine the light He has placed within you.

I love the quote by Marrianne Williamson that reads:

> "Our deepest fear is not that we are inadequate. Our deepest fear is that we are powerful beyond measure. It is our light, not our darkness that most frightens us. We ask ourselves, Who am I to be brilliant, gorgeous, talented, and fabulous? Actually, who are you not to be? You are a child of God. Your playing small does not serve the world. There is nothing enlightening about shrinking so that other people will not feel insecure around you. We are all meant to shine, as children do. We are born to make manifest the glory of God that is within us. It is not just in some of us; it is in everyone and as we let our own light shine, we unconsciously give others permission to do the same. As we are liberated from our own fear, our presence automatically liberates others."[72]

I dare you to liberate yourself. I dare you to use that liberation to lift others. We need you. The world needs you. I want to invite you to step up and take the space that is rightfully yours—space which no one else can fill.

Healing practices to adopt:

1. **Spend time imagining yourself at the end of your life.**

   Imagine yourself happy and proud of the things you have done. Who are you? What are you most proud of? What relationships thrived? What job did you have? What accomplishments did you slay? Write it all out if you can. Sometimes when I feel like I'm losing my way, I refer to this woman in my mind. She is a woman sitting in a chair, looking out her window and smiling. She is happy. I sometimes ask her questions. I ask her how she did it, and I try to live my life in a way that would bring her peace.

2. **Keep your mind open.**

When opportunities arise to try something new, try it! You don't know what you will end up liking or being good at. Everything new is uncomfortable. Embrace that it'll be scary and do it anyway! Go on the trip. Talk to different people. Eat the food. Ride the rides. Try new tricks. Jump off the cliffs and out of planes. Pick up the instruments that intrigue you. Learn the languages. Keep exploring life as if you were on a once-in-a-lifetime trip, for isn't that the truth?

3. **Share your gift in every stage of its development.**

Do you remember what cellphones used to look like? Do yourself a favor and go and take a Googly look at those bricks and have a good laugh! Can you imagine packing that thing around in your back pocket!? Now, have you ever wondered what would have happened if cell phone companies would have waited until they had perfected the smartphones we have today before sharing with the world what they had been working on back then?

First of all, they would have never gotten here! Their growth was catapulted by letting others use it. Second, what a waste of an incredible gift that millions around the world have benefitted from all this time! Have you realized that even big-name companies today don't wait until their phones are done? They release them and then update them later! Isn't that wild to think about? They aren't done, and they confidently release them anyway! I've learned a lot from that. I know firsthand that the pit of perfection is a hard one to crawl out of.

Many of my dreams have died in the pit of perfection. So I'm learning to do things differently now. I want to share like these companies; I want to share early, imperfectly, and confidently, allowing for improvements as I go.

You may very well have found flaws in this book. I'm sure you have because let's face it, I barely graduated high school! I'm sure they are here, but at some point, I had to make the decision to move forward anyway. I hoped that you would feel that the gift was worth the mistakes you see. If you have noticed my flaws, let them be a reminder to you that your gifts need not be perfect either. Your gift is worth giving to someone somewhere right now. As is. Imperfectly beautiful.

4. **Keep going.**

Once you've found your sweet spot, work at it until it can become your life's work. There is nothing wrong with doing what you love for a living. And if you're a woman, there is nothing wrong with your living creating a substantial amount of money for you and your family. We have spent too much time playing it small as if we don't deserve the same amount of success as our male counterparts. Your talents can bless lives as much as his. You deserve the peace and sense of security from knowing that no matter what happens in life, you can take care of yourself.

5. **Shine that beautiful light within you!**

17

THE MIRACLE OF HEALING

Whew! We made it through the 10! How are you doing? These 10 parts of you are each worth their own work, devotion, and time. I hope you're not overwhelmed. I want to remind you that healing is a process that evolves over time. There will be layers of healing and lessons to learn at different times in your life. Remember to be whole is not about perfection. Instead, it is about using our whole selves to go through life. It is about enjoying our pieces and using them to the best of our abilities.

Where to start.

So, where do you start this process?

The simple answer is—wherever you would like.

Pick one area at a time. Working on one will be more powerful than two. Each one deserves time to develop and grow strong. It is my hope that as you picked up this book and started reading that there was a specific chapter that seemed to stand out to you. Most likely you had already been longing for some help in a particular area. If you'd like to start there, set goals and grow until you're feeling better. I think that is great! Jump around as you please and as your life directs you. There is really no wrong way to go about picking up the pieces. You need only start and things will come together for you.

If you're someone who likes more structure, there are courses available on my site. In the main *Becoming Whole* course, I dedicate specific assignments for each 'part' of you. The course is meant to be an entire life overhaul, dramatically transforming the life you are currently living in a short amount of time. In this course, I take you by the hand and guide you through a thorough and do-able cleansing of your personal space, physical body, spiritual body, and mind. I will guide you through strengthening your voice, heart, gut, sexuality, relationships, and talents in ways I simply cannot not dive into in this book.

I have a workbook that allows you to set your own goals and track your own progress, taking the course over as you continue your upward spiral, becoming more whole day after day, year after year. These courses and further content is available at www.heatherfalter.com[73]

Otherwise, if you're a lone wolf, know that you've got this! Healing is possible and probable. Take your time getting to know yourself and each part of your life. Determine what needs your attention the most and start there. Do a personal inventory as often as you would like to see how things have changed and what part of you needs some extra love. Get professional help if you want it. Know that you are worth that help.

To all of you, whether you continue with me or not, please know that the different setbacks and struggles that you may have faced do not define you. They absolutely do not determine the amount of success or happiness available to you in your future. You undoubtedly deserve and can have JOY in all areas of your life. Will life be perfect? No. But you can experience gratitude, growth, and happiness *anyway*. Don't worry about where to start. Begin where you would like and go from there. Baby steps are bigger than you think. There is a magical upward spiral that begins when you set a goal and focus on one thing. One simple change for the better opens the doors for all areas of your life to improve. As stated previously, "A rising tide lifts all boats."[36] Getting up off the couch and making a decision to move forward *is* the rising tide.

The miracle of healing

All that is required for us to heal is to begin making the effort in the right direction, have faith, and keep going. It is very simple. While it's simple, I want to make it known that *these efforts we make are not what heals us.* All of the ointments, medicines, and remedies in the world are not what heals us. As with a broken plate that is shattered, super glue can only go so far. If we were left to our own devices when we fell and got cut, we could stitch it up. At best, we would get really good at stitching or gluing, but those stitches would remain forever. An open wound would never be undone.

The miracle of this life is that God knew when He created you that you would get hurt. He foresaw all of your wounds and created your body in a manner that it might heal itself through *His power.* His power is complete. The second you break a bone or puncture skin, your body begins to tend to the wound, protecting itself from outside ailments and instinctively working to create new cells, new life, and stronger tissue. The body, the mind, the spirit, they instinctively know what to do. You are a miracle. You were created by a miraculous being who loves you. He knew preventing you from every fall would not help you become strong, so He provided a way for you to recover. Your body, mind, and spirit are miracles that will heal through His power if you only gather up the pieces and try to put them where they go. This is the job you are asked to do. This is the level of faith you first need to extend. Then, when you have done all you can, your job is to be still and *watch as the Master that created you heals you.*

If you have overcome hard things, I want you to know that you are a symbolic witness that God exists. There is something beyond us all that cares for us, and you are living proof that there is more out there than what you see.

Tonight I opened my scriptures to a chapter that spoke of the terrible things that were done to our Savior. He was rejected and crucified. He was hated beyond measure for doing good and being good. And then I read this line, "and after he is laid in a sepulcher for the space of three days he shall rise from the dead, with healing in his wings."[74]

It gives me so much hope and encouragement knowing what Christ did with His Crucifixion. He *rose again*, with *healing in His wings*.

What will you do with your own personal crucifixion?

I hope you rise again. I can't think of anyone better to call upon for help than the One who knows the way. He quite literally already paved the path of healing for you.

Somehow Christ, with His healing wings, was able to meet me where I was at. He found *me*, a broken girl on the floor of her empty apartment. He took me by the hand and lovingly whispered, 'Heather, I'm here. I want to help you get back up.' He showed me one step at a time, nothing more, nothing less. He waited patiently as I fell, as I resisted, and as I mourned. It took time, but I slowly regained my trust in Him. We are still in this healing process together, and I still have no idea where we are going! But somehow, magically, as I reflect on my life, I can see that He has fixed what I could not fix. He healed wounds that I could not heal. He overcame what I could not overcome. And led me to a whole world so beautiful I could not have found it myself.

18

LIBERATING JOY

I f you continue, there will come a day where your life is completely unrecognizable. You will look back on your own experiences and remember your old life as if it were a dream. I believe there will come a time when nothing else remains of the old you except a few scars.

If you are left with scars, I hope you love them as much as I do! I hope you look at them and are reminded of your strength. I hope they remind you that no matter what you have been through or will go through, healing is possible. I hope they remind you that what once was thin and fragile is now strong. I hope they speak to you the truth that *you have overcome;* that you can do it again and again and again if life calls for it. But more than anything, I hope they remind you to be kind.

If there is one thing that makes going through hell worth it, it's the knowledge of what it's like to make it to the other side. You will one day hold within your heart and mind a jewel of knowledge and experience that someone else will need. I hope you share all of your jewels.

If is ever a tragedy after you figured out how to heal, it would be you not turning around to help another. I've asked myself, "Heather, If the lessons on how to overcome difficulty were born, lived, and died with you, what good were they?" I was worth it, yes, but I feel deep within my heart that my experiences were only the first step.

I believe it is our duty to help one another; to not let any experience go wasted. I hope that if nothing else comes from your past experiences, if you learn nothing else from me or this book or anyone else, ever, I hope you learn this one thing—compassion.

There will come a day where someone somewhere is in a similar situation to the one you have walked through. I hope that because of your life, you will have endless amounts of compassion for them. I hope you stand ready to comfort them and guide them through their pain the best you know how. I hope your eyes are opened to the many people out there who might be looking for help and I hope you help them.

We are surrounded by a whole world full of people who are suffering, who are searching for answers as to how to heal the wounds that a relentless world continues to inflict upon them. I can imagine as you've read this book, a person, or many people, have entered into your mind that might benefit from reading the words on these pages. I hope you give them a copy of this book. We need each other to get through this life and you never know who may be praying for help right now. Please be an answer to their prayers. Let them borrow your copy, tear out pages for them, whatever! I don't care how you do it, but I hope you think of them and I hope you share what you can to help those who are in your circle. You never know the friendship it may bring.

If you do not share it for *them*, I hope you at least *do it for yourself*. To think of someone struggling and to offer them relief will heal your own soul in ways you simply cannot in any other way. Doing this will help you grow. It will elevate your perspective, it will make your burdens seem light and it will bring a sense of peace and love into places of your heart that seemed like they would never feel again.

Your loneliness will ease. I promise you it works. Thinking of others will speed up your healing process.

I know you might feel nervous to reach out to someone in their time of need. We tend to feel inadequate when we want to help. I know. I feel it all the time! I don't know why we think that we need to have superpowers to do any good! We tend to wrongfully believe that our experiences are typical and our talent is under-qualified. I'll be honest, I've felt those feelings the entire time I have been writing this book! I worry about falling short, fumbling, and offending. I worry about it ALL. And then I remind myself that I'm going to show up as the woman who reaches out anyway. I remind myself that my heart is good even if I am the only one at the end of the day who knows that. I combat all of my worries by relying on grace to catch me, even if I fall.

I keep this quote on my phone and look at it often:

"To make a difference in someone's life you don't have to be brilliant, rich, beautiful, or perfect. You just have to care."
- Mandy Hale[75]

If you care, you're qualified to try. I personally believe that without compassion, you can have an okay life. I think you can have success and a lot of fun with that, but *true joy*, deep and lasting joy, will only come from this one quality. Your healing will not be complete until you learn to lift others. *I promise there is nothing more liberating than to turn your darkest night into someone's north star.* In these moments of lifting another, you will recognize that everything you have been through was worth it.

There is a book called *For the Love* by Jen Hatmaker. In it she says:

"I pray for your kindness more than your success, because the latter without the former is a tragedy. God measures our entire existence by only two things - how we love Him and how we love people. If you get this right, you can get a million other things wrong."[76]

As this book comes to a close, I pray that you have found hope in healing. I hope you always remember that the possibilities for your future are beyond your comprehension and imagination. I truly believe that there are things in store for you—friendships, relationships, and experiences that you could never predict in your wildest dreams. Opportunities await you. Happiness and true joy await you. Please believe that.

I promise you there will come a day when you look back on your life and all you've been through with awe and gratitude. There will come a day when you are no longer burdened by the weight of life's sorrows. There will come a day when you think of the hard times and wouldn't trade a second of it, because of what it has made of you. There will come a day where you don't even recognize your new self because of the strength you now have.

There will also come a day when someone, somewhere, has been through something similar. Because of your life, you will have endless amounts of compassion. You will see yourself in him or her. You will also have walked your own path with the Savior for so long, you will begin to mimic Him as you lift another. Your heart will ache as you hear their story. You will stand with them as they mourn and comfort them with the deepest level of comfort. You will be able to identify where they are hurting and strengthen where they are weak. One by one, you will help them pick up piece by broken piece, offering each one to the Savior, asking what to do with that specific piece.

Finally, you will know that through your pain, God has given you a taste of His love. It is a special and tender love that burns especially strong for anyone struggling.

ACKNOWLEDGEMENTS

First, I need to thank God for the life I have been given. He knew the life I would need to become who I am, and He loved me enough to give it to me. His hands are the hands that have carried me. His voice is the voice that whispers in the night.

I want to thank both of my parents for giving me a beautiful life, and for raising me up with all the love they both had to give. I love you both and know that I am who I am because you set me free. Thank you for encouraging me to be the best I can be.

Mom, thank you for fighting through your hurt, and rising up like the warrior you are. I'm proud to be your daughter, and am in continual awe by the obstacles you have unfailingly overcome. You are my hero, and *I'll love you forever*.

Dad, thank you for calling me more! I have loved our conversations lately! I'm so proud to be raised a Moss, and so proud to be your daughter.

To my siblings, thank you for filling my life up with SO MUCH JOY. Your love and friendship mean the world to me. Every one of you is my favorite! Thank you, each of you, for being yourselves. You're all so freaking cool in your own way!

To my husband, Travis. I don't know how you were crazy enough to marry me! But I need you to know that no other person on earth has felt more like my Savior than you. I walked into your life as a broken girl, and your soothing presence has calmed the storms within my soul. I thank

God we crossed each other's paths, chose to create a life together, and made a couple of gorgeous babies! You three have become my best friends.

To my babies who will forever be my "babies", Avenlei and Parx. God picked the best to be mine! I don't know how on earth I got the sweetest babies, but I did. You kiddos light up my life and give it so much purpose!

Thank you to my 'soul' friends: Cori Johnson, Jessica Lagerquist, Alina Dyhre, Melissa Lowe, Josh Mojica, Aleisha Christensen, Savannah McGary, Dani Falter, Wendy Rice, Cicily Seamons, and TediRae Edwards. You are all my angels on earth. I have each of your names etched upon my heart.

And finally, thank you to my mentors: Brandon Falter, Ryan Harris, and Alene Kovac.

I am the luckiest.

- Heather

ENDNOTES

1   Heather Falter. "Home Page." HeatherFalter.com 2020, www. heatherfalter.com

2   The Book of Mormon. Ed. Church of Jesus Christ of Latter-day Saints. Salt Lake City: Church of Jesus Christ of Latter-day Saints, 2006. Print.

3   The Book of Mormon (see Reference #2), 2 Nephi 2:25

4   The Book of Mormon (see Reference #2), 1 Nephi 2:1, 2 Nephi 5:1-5, 2 Nephi 25:12-13, Mosiah 24:11-15

5   The Book of Mormon (see Reference #2), Alma 14:6-11

6   The Book of Mormon (see Reference #2), Stories found all throughout. See Second Nephi 2: 27-28, Ether 8:26, Moroni 9:6

7   The Book of Mormon (see Reference #2), Alma 5:28, Helaman 12:5, Mosiah 27:3-5, Alma 30:11

8   Byron Katie, "Home Page" The Work Of Byron Katie, 2020. thework.com

9   Moana. 2016. [DVD] Directed by Ron Clements and John Musker U.S: Walt Disney Pictures.

10 Byron Katie with Stephen Mitchell. Loving What Is: Four Questions That Can Change Your Life. Harmony; Reprint edition. May 7, 2002

11 Byron Katie, "Home Page" The Work Of Byron Katie, 2020. thework.com

12 How Far I'll Go, Write and produced by Lin-Manuel Miranda, Performed by Auli'i Cravalho and Alessia Cara. Moana. 2016:Walt Disney Pictures

13   Marie Mongan. Hypnobirthing: The Breakthrough To Safer, Easier, More Comfortable Childbirth. Health Communications Inc; Updated edition. December 8, 2015

14   Glennon Doyle Melton. Love Warrior. Flatiron Books; First Edition edition (September 6, 2016)

15   Heather Falter. "Home Page." HeatherFalter.com 2020, www.heatherfalter.com

16   Heather Falter. "How I Found Emotional Healing Through Honest Creativity." Apr 13, 2018. TEDxIdahoFalls Video, 16:05, https://youtu.be/BzICMuTqhaA

17   Doug Manning. Don't Take My Grief Away From Me:How to Walk Through Grief and Learn to Live Again 3rd Edition. In Sight Books; 3 edition (September 15, 2011)

18   C.S. Lewis. Mere Christianity. HarperOne; Revised & Enlarged edition (May 28, 2009)

19   Oprah Winfrey. "Oprah's Favorite Definition of Forgiveness | SuperSoul Sunday | Oprah Winfrey Network" Mar 15, 2018. SuperSoul Sunday, Oprah Winfrey Network Youtube Video, 1:16, https://youtu.be/y-7p4gfVt6w

20   The Book Of Mormon: Another Testament Of Jesus Christ (See Reference #2) 2 Nephi 2:6-7,26; Mosiah 15:6–27;

21   KJV, Matthew 5:18; The Book Of Mormon: Another Testament Of Jesus Christ (See Reference #2) 3 Nephi 1:25

22   KJV, Mark 10:21; The Book Of Mormon: Another Testament Of Jesus Christ (See Reference #2) Enos 1:27

23   unknown artist and source

24   Strider Sports International, Inc. Rapid City, SD. 2020. www.striderbikes.com

25   Brian Pickett. "Keep Trying". © 2012 The Fred Rogers Company. Daniel Tiger www.pbskids.org/daniel

26   Gilbert, Elizabeth. Eat, Pray, Love: One Woman's Search for Everything Across Italy, India and Indonesia. Directed by Ryan Murphy. Movie tie-in ed. New York: Penguin, 2010.

27   Moana. 2016. Directed by R. Clements. DVD. U.S: Walt Disney Pictures.

28   Calee Reed. Cleanse You. 3:37 Released: February 9, 2018 ℗ 2018 Shadow Mountain Records

29   Gilbert, Elizabeth. Eat, Pray, Love: One Woman's Search for Everything Across Italy, India and Indonesia. Directed by Ryan Murphy. Movie tie-in ed. New York: Penguin, 2010

30   Glennon Doyle Melton. Love Warrior. Flatiron Books; First Edition edition (September 6, 2016)

31   I have looked endlessly for this story. I cannot find it anywhere! If anyone knows of this story so that I can reference it properly, please send me the info to heather@heatherfalter.co

32   The Book Of Mormon: Another Testament Of Jesus Christ (See Reference #2) 2 Nephi 2:25

33   Heather Falter, "It Is I" A painting of Christ's eyes. www.heatherfalter.com

34   Instructed by Joeel & Natalie Rivera and Victoria Hawkins. udemy.com. Therapeutic Art Life Coach Certification. Module #36 Looking at Ourselves as a Whole Person. 8 min. 2020 Udemy, Inc. https://www.udemy.com/course/art-therapy-life-coach-certification/ Their original list is as follows: Physical Body, Energetic Aura, Personal Space, Mental, Self-expression, Emotional/Feelings, Spiritual/Intuition.

35   Taken from wikipedia.com: "The phrase is commonly attributed to John F Kennedy,[1] who used it in a 1963 speech to combat criticisms that a dam project he was inaugurating was a pork barrel project.[2][3] However, in his memoir Counselor: A Life At The Edge Of History, Kennedy's speechwriter Ted Sorensen revealed that the phrase was not one of his or the then President's own fashioning. It was in Sorensen's first year working for him, during Kennedy's tenure in the Senate, when Sorensen was trying to tackle economic problems in New England, that he happened upon the phrase. He wrote that he noticed that "the regional chamber of commerce, the New England Council, had a thoughtful slogan: 'A rising tide lifts all the boats.'" From then on, Kennedy would borrow the slogan often. Sorensen highlighted this as an example of quotes mistakenly attributed to President Kennedy.[4]" wikipedia.org. "A rising tide lifts all boats." last edited

on 14 April 2020. Wikipedia® is a registered trademark of the Wikimedia Foundation, Inc., a non-profit organization. https://en.wikipedia.org/wiki/A_rising_tide_lifts_all_boats

36 Marie Kondo. The Life-Changing Magic of Tidying Up: The Japanese Art of Decluttering and Organizing. Ten Speed Press; 1st edition (October 14, 2014)

37 Anthony William. Medical Medium: Secrets Behind Chronic and Mystery Illness and How to Finally Heal. Hay House Inc.; Later Printing Used edition (November 10, 2015)

38 Anthony William. Medical Medium. Visit the "About Page" on www.medicalmedium.com. https://www.medicalmedium.com/medical-medium-about-anthony-william Other books: Live Changing Foods, Thyroid Healing, Liver Rescue, Celery Juice, Cleanse to Heal

39 Melissa Hartwig. The Whole30's Food Freedom Forever: Letting Go of Bad Habits, Guilt, and Anxiety Around Food. Houghton Mifflin Harcourt; 1 edition (October 4, 2016)

40 wikipedia.org. "Phantom Pain". Last Edited:15 April 2020. https://en.wikipedia.org/wiki/Phantom_pain

41 The Utah College of Massage Therapy, Lindon, Utah Campus.

42 Elder Peter M. Johnson. Power to Overcome the Adversary. October 2019 General Conference talk. Sunday Afternoon Session. https://www.churchofjesuschrist.org/study/general-conference/2019/10/54johnson?lang=eng

43 The Book Of Mormon: Another Testament Of Jesus Christ (See Reference #2) 2 Nephi 28:22

44 KJV James 4:7

45 For more information visit: Heather Falter. "Home Page." HeatherFalter.com 2020, www.heatherfalter.com or TEDxIdahoFalls talk Heather Falter. "How I Found Emotional Healing Through Honest Creativity." Apr 13, 2018. TEDxIdahoFalls Video, 16:05, https://youtu.be/BzICMuTqhaA

46 Ryan Holiday, Stillness Is the Key. Portfolio (October 1, 2019)

47 Rhonda Byrne. The Magic (The Secret Book 3). Atria Books (March 6, 2012)

48 Brooke Castillo. The Life Coach School Podcast. 2020 https:// thelifecoachschool.com/podcasts/

49 I highly recommend faith-based hypnotherapists from the Certified Hypnotherapy Training School. Farr West, UT. Visit certifiedhypnotherapytrainingschool.com

50 Dr. Marlo Archer. Maybe so, Maybe Not, We'll See. 2020 - Dr. Marlo Archer. Down to Earth Enterprises. http://www.drmarlo. com/dr-marlo-speaks/maybe-so-maybe-not-well-see/

51 en.wikipedia.org. "List of countries by life expectancy" last edited on 10 May 2020 https://en.wikipedia.org/wiki/ List_of_countries_by_life_expectancy.

52 Anthony William. Medical Medium. "Souls Gold" 55:11 2018. Soundcloud.com https://soundcloud.com/medicalmedium/ souls-gold

53 Garson O'Toole. Quote Investigator. "What You Do Speaks So Loudly that I Cannot Hear What You Say" 2011. www.quoteinvestigator.com https://quoteinvestigator. com/2011/01/27/what-you-do-speaks/

54 KJV. Proverbs 29:11

55 Rollin McCraty, Ph.D. Heart-Brain Neurodynamics: The Making of Emotions. Research Library Publication. Published: 2015. 2020 HeartMath Institute. heartmath.org (www.consciouslifestylemag. com/heart-intelligence/ & https://www.heartmath.org/ research/research-library/basic/heart-brain-neurodynamics/).

56 Robert Vallett, unknown source.

57 Rupi Kaur. The Sun and Her Flowers. Pg 109. Andrews McMeel Publishing; 1st edition (September 24, 2019)

58 Serge Geffrard, MD. The Amazing Human Heart. Children's Heart Specialists of Georgia. 2020. childrensheartga.com. (childrensheartga.com/amazing-facts-about-the-human-heart)

59 Mike Mcrae. Do We Really Only Get a Certain Number of Heartbeats in a Lifetime? Here's What Science Says. 14 APRIL 2018. sciencealert.com. (www.sciencealert.com/ relationship-between-heart-beat-and-life-expectancy/amp)

60 Jeffrey R. Holland. President Thomas S. Monson: Always on the Lord's Errand. November 1986. TheChurchOfJesusChrist.

Org https://www.churchofjesuschrist.org/study/
liahona/1986/10/president-thomas-s-monson-always-o
n-the-lords-errand?lang=eng

61 Dr. Jennifer Finlayson Fife. https://www.finlayson-fife.com/ Quote
posted on instagram September 23, 2020 @finlaysonfife https://
www.instagram.com/p/CFfs834Bf5W/?igshid=1fss16extspf3

62 I first heard of this concept from Sabrina Lynn's Podcast
ReWilding for Women. Episode # 92 Sacred Sexuality:
Reclaiming the Forbidden with the Dark Goddess & Dark God.
The concept is found at approximately 26 minutes. https://
podcasts.apple.com/us/podcast/rewilding-for-women/
id1151621599?i=1000475840664

63 Heather Falter. www.heatherfalter.com.

64 A religious leader I met once and never learned his name! (This
is proof that you never know the good you do.)

65 Jed Diamond. The 5 Stages of Love: Why Too Many Stop at
Stage 3. August 6, 2015. menalive.com https://menalive.com/
stages-of-love/

66 Mother Teresa. Reportedly inscribed on the wall of Mother
Teresa's children's home in Calcutta, and attributed to her.

67 Heather Falter. www.heatherfalter.com/blog

68 Alice Jo Pierson Miner. Personal Message on March 21, 2020

69 Rhonda Byrne. The Magic (The Secret Book 3). Atria Books
(March 6, 2012)

70 Source unknown.

71 Steve Jobs. Steve Jobs' Stanford Commencement address on
June 12, 2005. Video found at news.stanford.edu. https://news.
stanford.edu/2005/06/14/jobs-061505/

72 Mirrianne Williamson. A Return to Love: Reflections on the
Principles of "A Course in Miracles" HarperOne; Reissue edition
(March 15, 1996)

73 Heather Falter. "Home Page." HeatherFalter.com 2020, www.
heatherfalter.com

74 The Book Of Mormon: Another Testament Of Jesus Christ (See
Reference #2) 2 Nephi 25:12-13

75   Mandy Hale. The Single Woman: Life, Love, and a Dash of Sass. Thomas Nelson; 6/29/13 edition (August 13, 2013) Mandyhale.com
76   Jen Hatmaker. For the Love: Fighting for Grace in a World of Impossible Standards. Thomas Nelson (August 18, 2015)

ABOUT THE AUTHOR

Heather Falter is an Artist, Author, Blogger, and Course Instructor. Her work is primarily based on helping you to embrace your own healing after tragedy and heartache. She teaches you how to grieve properly, find forgiveness, and claim joy again. She acknowledges that you have a unique voice and a unique path to finding your highest self. She is fiercely devoted to honoring whichever path you choose, encouraging you to climb back into  the driver's seat of your own life. You have desires. You have dreams for yourself. You have unique gifts and talents. She helps you to overcome whatever heartaches you might be facing right now in order to claim your highest potential as your new reality.

Heather, her husband, and her two kids live in Idaho, USA.

HELPING YOU HEAL YOUR LIFE
ONE PIECE AT A TIME

NO MATTER HOW BROKEN YOU MAY FEEL OR HOW MESSY YOUR LIFE IS RIGHT
NOW, I WANT YOU TO KNOW THAT YOU CAN HEAL. WHATEVER YOU ARE GOING
THROUGH—WHETHER IT BE DIVORCE, FINANCIAL RUIN, SICKNESS, THE DEATH OF
A LOVED ONE, A NATURAL DISASTER, ETC. HEATHER FALTER WILL GENTLY GUIDE
YOU THROUGH THE WORK OF GRIEF, FORGIVENESS AND ACCEPTANCE.

IN THIS BOOK, YOU WILL LOOK AT ALL THE PIECES THAT
MAKE UP THE WHOLE OF YOU, INCLUDING:

- PERSONAL SPACE
- PHYSICAL BODY
- SPIRITUAL BODY
- MIND
- VOICE

- HEART
- INTUITION
- SEXUALITY
- RELATIONSHIPS
- TALENTS

AS YOU PICK UP EACH PIECE AND INCORPORATE HEATHER'S
DIVINELY INSPIRED HEALING PRACTICES, YOUR LIFE WILL BEGIN
TO OVERFLOW WITH JOY. YOU WILL HEAL FROM YOUR PAIN,
AND YOU WILL BECOME WHO YOU WERE BORN TO BE.

ARE YOU READY?

BECOMING WHOLE

HEATHER
FALTER

BECOMING WHOLE

HOW TO PICK UP YOUR BROKEN PIECES AND
BE WHO YOU WERE BORN TO BE

HEATHER FALTER

For Artwork (including the cover of this book),
meditations, therapeutic art classes and Becoming
Whole courses, coaching, interviews, and public speaking
inquiries,
visit www.heatherfalter.com
To connect: scan the code below with your smartphone
camera.

Made in the USA
Monee, IL
15 January 2021